ECSTATIC
BELONGING

A YEAR ON THE MEDICINE PATH

Caffyn Jesse

Second 2024 Edition.
Copyright © 2024 by Caffyn Jesse

cover photo: Roosting Monarch Butterflies
during migration by Jessica Bolser/USFWS

Electronic book: ISBN 978-0-9738332-7-0
Paperback book: ISBN 978-1-7381211-2-0

Book Layout: Ravi Ramgati

TABLE OF CONTENTS

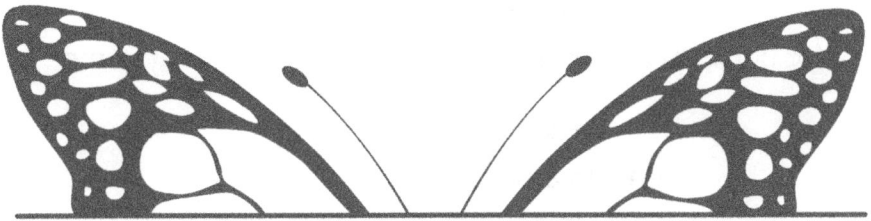

INTRODUCTION

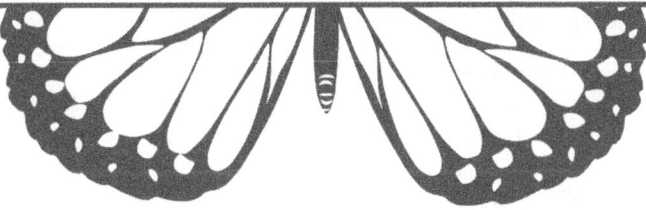

*Come walk the medicine
path with me.*

Can we learn to live and die in ever-better love,
instead of being ruled by fear?
Can we find transpersonal belonging ecstatically,
instead of traumatically?

By reconnecting ecstasy with equilibrium,
we find a truing mechanism
for personal and interpersonal neuroendocrine systems.

And magic can happen.
We already know this to be true.

The universe is magic.
According to the laws of physics, all this should not exist.

The biosphere is queer and unpredictable.
The singular one of you is powerful magic too.
I see you: rule-breaker; lovemaker.

Let me make love with you.
Let's fight capitalism and colonialism
with our wild imaginations, loving touch and daring dreams.

We can make space and time,
for even more magic.

What if we get this right?
Let's dive in, and share delight!

THE MEDICINE PATH OF EMBODIED LOVE

There is a medicine path of embodied love I want to share with you. On this path, we commit to our own souls and feel them amplified, as we join in intimate connection with one another. Integrity grows in the experience of deep, abiding intimacies, resourced by many experiences of ecstasy.

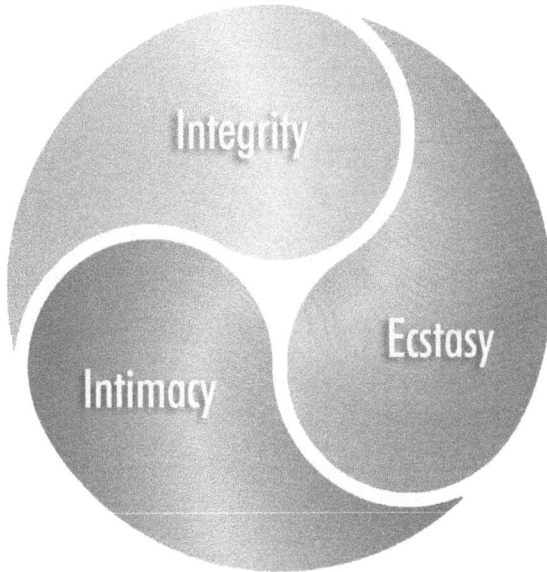

Embodied love is everywhere, within and around us, but we aren't trained to know and grow it. We live and die as parched versions of ourselves, without its guiding gifts. Epidemic levels of social isolation and loneliness are affecting people's physical and mental health, across the world. Our disconnection from each other feeds the politics of hate. It undergirds economies of fear, generating cascades of catastrophic consequences. Crisis after crisis, we problem-solve, with increasing urgency and mounting hopelessness.

We know it should be different. Moreover, many of us experience rare moments when we feel profoundly different. Through many different practices, we harvest moments of expanded awareness. A sense of ecstatic belonging emerges, and feels like home. For precious moments, we are at one with ourselves, each other, and all life.

Psychedelic medicine and erotic practice are ways I reliably find the homecoming of ecstatic belonging. Others find it through activism, artmaking, sweat lodges, forest bathing, music, dance, meditation, community celebration, lovemaking, ninety recovery meetings in ninety days.... There are many ways we access an embodied experience of love, and transpersonal unity. We are taught to frame our moments of ecstatic belonging as occasional, extraordinary experiences; we return then to "real life" and its urgencies. What if instead we choose to really pay attention to our ecstasies, and root our lives and loves in them? I will explain how, in the science of nervous systems and ecosystems, ecstasies serve as truing mechanisms. Ecstatic practice helps us weave loving intimacies and supportive communities. We are inventing and living powerful alternatives to capitalism and colonialism, with our wild imaginations, loving touch and daring dreams.

"Ecstatic Belonging" is the theme that focuses my personal explorations, as I walk my own medicine path. Different aspects of ecstatic belonging support one another, and deepening into the differences sequentially feels enriching. The calendar I suggest here is a rhythm I can dance to, in my own ongoing learning. Certain psychedelic medicines, exercises and erotic practices feel best, as I dive into different aspects of ecstatic belonging. In the science of stardust, cells and soils, there are

stories to inspire. There is poetry, too, in this more beautiful world that is both ancient and new. Ecstatic Belonging is a way of life I practice. I invite you to join me, in whatever particular way can work for you. What is your medicine path? How do you find and feel embodied love? What is your ecstatic practice?

Whatever month you come upon this offering, you are welcome to join me in my rhythm. Or you can make your own desire lines through the text, and generate your own rhythm. Take what you like, and leave the rest.

Six Steps to Ecstatic Belonging

Ecstatic belonging is a climax state that keeps emerging, on the medicine path of embodied love. The path itself is sometimes joyful, and sometimes tortuous. Through challenges and delights, these are the steps I want to keep on taking, simultaneously and sequentially:

1. I belong to my own soul. I surrender to the ever-emerging truth of me. I know it and grow it.
2. I belong to those I love. I practice welcoming and cherishing them, including their unlovable parts.
3. I want ecstasy, and I commit to belonging to my longing.
4. I belong to the biosphere that lives through me.
5. I belong to repair. I commit to repairing harm I have done, whether intentionally or unintentionally. I commit to repairing harm done to me.
6. I belong to nonbeing. I integrate spaciousness, as I weave my self into the web of life and death.

This is the calendar I loosely follow. In each 2-month period I have specific psychedelic medicines, exercises and erotic practices to resource my inquiry.

January & February: Belonging to Our Souls
There is a belonging that no tyrant can take from us.
There is only one me. There is only one you. How can I
better discern and follow my own soul's calling?

March and April: Belonging to Each Other
We can fail each other, and disappoint ourselves,
and still reach for more and better love. There are
medicines and practices to guide us.

May and June: Belonging to Ecstasy
We can learn from the more-than-human world, and
from the stardust, cells and soils of us, to belong to our
longing for ecstasy, and build capacities for expanded
ecstatic states.

July and August: Belonging to Interbeing
We can choose interbeing, and join the more-than-
human world in its wild wisdoms, so we feel the
companionship of others, lovers and ancestors, in the
web of life and death.

September and October: Belonging to Repair
We can learn to belong to repair, as we orient to
healing harm we have done, and experienced.

November and December: Belonging to Nonbeing
We can explore and ally with the spaciousness of
nonbeing, within and around us, as we practice dying.

RESONANCE

The medicine path of embodied love is a path of connection, care and mutual empowerment that works through resonance. When we feel resonance with another or others, there is amplification of our own vibration. We find deep, sustaining pleasure. Interactions between resonant frequencies allow for the generation and storage of vibrational energy.

Resonance is an emergent property of systems at a vast range of spatial scales, from sub-atomic particles to relationships between stars. We share a longing for resonance – within us, between us. If we let that longing exist, and give it our attention, it will guide us home. There is a science to this energy-generating system, which I share more of in my book *Love and Death in a Queer Universe*. In the book you are now reading, I share how feeling and finding my way to resonance is my ongoing inquiry.

Resonant relationships are generative. They open new dimensions of me and you. They let us settle into the singularity I am and you are, and co-create just-this-one of us, that we can only be together. Singularity, anchored in a resilient web of belonging, gets deepened in its dignity. Belonging, manifested through intricate intimacies between resonant singularities, gets evermore power and truth.

With resonance, two is more than one plus one. We exit linear time, where addition is simple. We bid goodbye to the heteronormative world of either-or. The weave of us is more than the sum of us. With resonance, we contradict the laws of physics. An energy unique to us is generated. This happens at every level of existence: quarks, atoms, molecules, microtubules, cells, ecosystems, solar systems and social systems. Reaching out from the truth of enhanced stability and empowerment, we can feel and find our way to other resonant intimacies, and communal ecstasies. Through resonance, we actually, literally *generate* a power greater than ourselves.

We live at a time when systems of capitalism and colonialism have global domination – and it is a time of mass extinction, climate chaos and social crisis. In the face of all the relentless daily violences, what do we attend? Can we learn to love each other with wild wisdoms, as the world ends? Do we dare to grieve all that is lost, through every agonizing extinction, while we still take time to rest – and savour the beauty and magic that remains?

Dare we follow the longing for resonance, within and between us? Dare we feel how that same longing organizes the quarks, atoms, cells, soils and souls of us? Have we courage? Have we companionship? In the weave of us, each ecstasy can say Yes! to what we dare to dream of. Each experience of resonance plugs us into power.

The first law of thermodynamics – the Conservation of Energy – describes a hostile universe, [1] where energy is scarce. According to this law, the total amount of energy in the universe remains the same. We should try to enclose and exploit all the energy we can, then, because if you get more, I get less. There is danger everywhere. In this world, plants turn black by gobbling up all the energy. 1% of humans grow ever- richer, at the biosphere's expense. Through resonance, we inhabit a friendly universe, where there is abundance. Energy

---

1   Through this paragraph I am referring to Albert Einstein's reflection "I think the most important question facing humanity is, 'Is the universe a friendly place?' This is the first and most basic question all people must answer for themselves."

is co-created, as an emergent property of relationship, at every level – quantum, cellular, ecosystem and biosphere. Plants turn green, as they take and create energy. There is plenty to give away. By aligning our cells, souls and social world with the consciousness of stardust, plants and ecosystems, we generate power.

Resonance exceeds all laws. It cannot be regulated, commanded, enclosed or exploited. Because it only, always comes into being as an emergent property of relational systems, resonance can never be extinguished.

IMAGINAL COMMUNITY

I invite you to join me in a community of practice that exists only in our imaginations. Come play with me, outside of ordinary mind and linear time. We can be like imaginal cells that grow at the edges of an insect larva, imagining the beauty that can emerge from the molecular soup of death and disintegration, as the world ends.[2] In insect metamorphosis, imaginal cells get activated when an insect larva pupates. As the larval form of life dies and dissolves, these cells begin to resonate with one another. They reach for connection, until they form into the exoskeleton of an adult insect. A new, unpredictable form of life comes into being, in the face of certain death.

We can potentially access this kind of counternormative consciousness – when we are in ritual space with psychedelic medicines, immersed in passionate pursuits, or savouring post-orgasmic bliss. A spacious, non-linear time-inside-time opens

---

2   This idea comes from multi-disciplinary artist and cultural provocateur Alixa Garcia

up, and there is time to listen to the embodied wisdom within and between us. Attuning to the more-than-human world, we can find resonance within ourselves, and with each other.

We can reach together, then, for otherwise unknowable ecstasies, as we find welcome for our singular souls and skins. There is magic here. We can find ways to decohere love and fear, and support one another to choose love.

REWILDING AWARENESS

On the medicine path of embodied love, we need ongoing practices of rewilding awareness, so we don't stay in thrall to the hypnotic normal. Normative belonging is always precarious; it is earned by sacrifice and service, or secured by domination and control.

For me, psychedelic medicines are allies in rewilding awareness. These medicines change neuron connectivity, and transform the way brain systems synchronize. When our brains' subcritical "Default Mode Network" is exceeded, we access a more critical, creative awareness – what I describe as "Wild Mind." Neuroplasticity is amplified; dendrites on neurons get multiplied.

Psychedelic medicines are known to be effective at the level of individual healing, addressing Post-Traumatic Stress Disorder, depression, anxiety and fear of death. I believe we can co-create ways for these medicines to resource the work of social and environmental justice. They can help us find and practice enduring love. With the support of psychedelic medicines, we can become brave enough to lean into our longings for ecstatic belonging, even in the ongoing trauma, grief and terror of all the true dangers we are living and dying in.

I am committed to an ongoing, embodied practice of reaching for the ecstatic dimensions of my loving. I will share how I use ritual as a way to welcome intimacy, ecstasy and integrity into my relationships. In regular rituals I co-create with friends, we sometimes integrate psycholitic doses of psychedelic medicines, to resource us in belonging to each other.

Psychedelic medicines help us open doors that have rusted shut, but they come with real risks. Using psychedelics certainly isn't necessary. Many people don't want to work with medicines, or don't have safe access to them. Whether or not we integrate the use of psychedelics into our lives and relationships, a commitment to rewilding awareness is supported by other body-based practices.

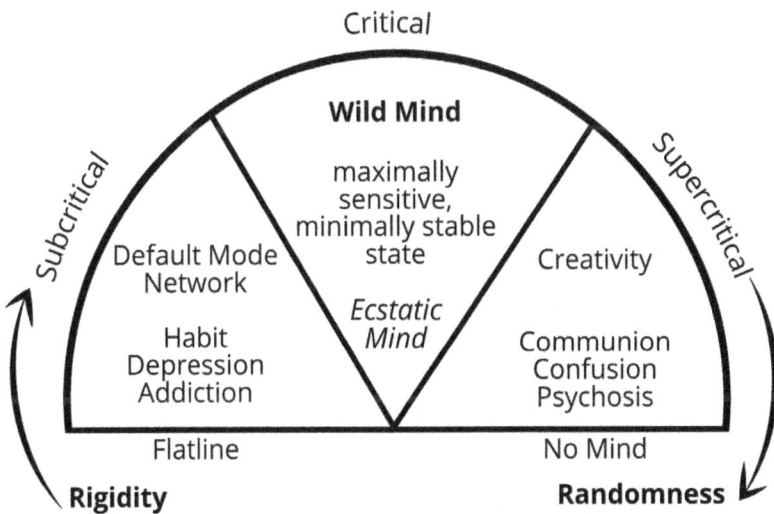

Figure: Wild Mind hovers in criticality, where new possibilities are ever-emerging

ECSTATIC PRACTICE

Conscious breathing, mindful erotic practice and erotic massage all foster similar neuroendocrine shifts to those we can find through psychedelic medicines. Stretching our bodies and souls into brave learning, we expand what is possible. For many years I have worked as a practitioner and teacher sacred intimacy, developing embodiment practices and erotic practices that might resource us. We can use various ecstatic practices to tune into the living world that lives in our bodies. We can viscerally experience somatic openings that locate us at the intersection of sex and spirit. These rich and multifaceted practices deepen their impact over time.

But please be careful! In ecstasy, we are likely to feel a sense of exceeding our singular selves. It can be joyful to experience a transpersonal unity with all life, or simply terrifying. For people who have not developed capacity for this experience, the self-abandonment of ecstasy can feel profoundly unsafe. It might trigger memories of how, during terrible experiences of trauma, we experience dissociative self-abandonment. In the imaginal community I invite, I imagine we are:

- choosing and cultivating the joyful self-leaving we feel and find, in experiences of ecstatic belonging
- distinguishing this from the terrible self-leaving we feel and find, in despair, and the dissociative self-abandonment of trauma
- finding ways to weave despair with ecstasy, so we can fully inhabit our personal and interpersonal neuroendocrine system

This is the is the work and play I want to share with you. We can belong to each other, and the process.

AN IMPORTANT NOTE ON THE NEURAL LEARNING ZONE

There is a well-known biological principle: too much stress is harmful. Trauma and chronic stress literally, biophysically damage cells, and impair the functioning of nervous systems. Too-little stress is just as harmful; it leads to nervous system atrophy. There is a place of just-right stress that supports the growth and strength of any organism. I call it the personal neural learning zone. The same principle applies in our relationships with one another. There is a place of just-enough stress that is our interpersonal learning zone, where we can be in the embodied learning of even-better love.

In what I share here, I describe how I work with different psychedelic medicine practices, erotic practices, and generative conflict practices. I don't recommend these practices for everybody, nor describe all the necessary precautions. There may be many good reasons not to do what I do! Medicines are powerful, and we need to learn their ways with reliable guides. Readers may have disabilities that make a particular practice irrelevant. Any practice might be too dangerous, triggering trauma responses that make it impossible for learning to emerge. Or a practice can be too pedestrian for you – far too boring to foster nervous system growth. We may be navigating power dynamics or abusive relationships that make certain practices unwise or impossible.

We can learn to work and play in our personal and interpersonal neural learning zones, by noticing when we get uncomfortable, but not unsafe. Then we need to get brave and resourced enough to choose discomfort, and welcome neurological change. But check the ripcord on your parachute, before you jump.

When working with psychedelic medicines and ecstatic practices, we expand our limits and dissolve our boundaries. It's important not to exceed what our sober neuroendocrine system has capacity to integrate. Clear discussion of fears, desires, boundaries, intentions, disabilities, limits and power dynamics before a ritual helps to create space where we are safe enough to be brave.

Any practice I describe can be done in your imagination, or actually. Imagining doing something new lights up new neural pathways, creating biophysical resource for doing something actual.

After brave learning experiences, we need time for rest, and savouring satisfactions. That is the space of neural rewiring and biophysical change, where new learning becomes embodied.

There are two branches of the autonomic nervous system; our neural learning zone has both sympathetic and parasympathetic components. The sympathetic branch of our autonomic nervous system (SNS) guides our excited, "awake and take" energies. Too much SNS activation becomes "fight or flight" energy – it feels like corrosive fear. But with too little brave excitement, we go flat and wither. The parasympathetic branch of our autonomic nervous system (PNS) guides our peaceful, "rest and digest" energies. Too little PNS activation means we are ever-anxious; we never rest and feel deeply satisfied. Too much PNS activation means we are over-attached to feeling safe; our nervous systems atrophy. Between too much and too little activation in both branches of our autonomic nervous system, there is an ever-changing neural learning zone where love can grow. A commitment to the path of embodied love keeps us in the ever-imperfect practice of learning both courage and serenity.

Every one of us needs to track our personal neural learning zone. How you engage with these materials can be guided by your ongoing inquiry. Please pick or invent the practices that are brave and safe enough for you! We can honour neurodiversity, and support each other in growing competencies, while learning to move at the pace of trust. Bravely trying things on, making mistakes, resting awhile and making repair are all part of inhabiting our personal and interpersonal neural learning zones.

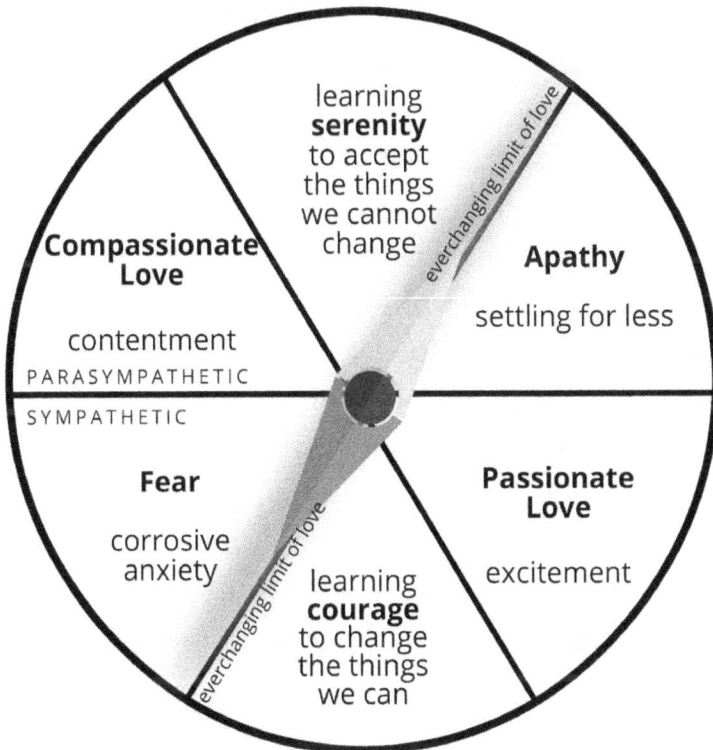

The neural learning zones of the sympathetic and parasympathetic branches of our autonomic nervous system, visualized as the limit of love.

I am Not a Teacher Here

It feels important to say I am not a teacher here. I am a fellow explorer on the medicine path. I am a would-be lover, offering my own understandings and practices as a reach for companionship, on my journey as a queer elder and advocate of embodied love.

I hope you will let this book love you. I hope that you find something here that meets with you, and encourages you to grow your singular self, and know your unmet need for ecstatic belonging. And I hope you will let my love fail you. As you notice the failures and inadequacies of my imperfect love, I invite your indignation. May our frustrations engorge our longings, and empower our reach, so we each find our way to the particular loves that are just right for us.

I find joy and excitement on this path of embodied love. In moments of ecstatic belonging, I find serenity and certainty. My longing for belonging guides me home, again and again – even in the midst of the world's bad news. The particles of us, and the biotic systems we partake of, already know how to do this. Ecstatic belonging is ever-emergent, at every level. It is submolecular, in the hadrons and atoms of us. It is metabolic. It's in our DNA. It guides our multicellular existence. It is ever-emergent in ecosystems.

Come walk the medicine path with me. If we walk the path of embodied love – separately and together – our fear can get right-size. We can heal the impact of trauma. We can meet ongoing traumas with more resource, together, instead of further traumatizing one another. We can make mistakes and find repair. We can join with the more-than-human world, and learn its love languages. What you bring to this path matters as much as what I bring. There are no competencies we need to manifest, to join this inquiry; there are no incompetencies we need to hide. We can belong to ourselves, each other and the process.

JANUARY AND FEBRUARY: BELONGING TO OUR SOULS

I belong to my own soul.
I surrender to the ever-emerging truth of me.
I know it and grow it.

Belonging to Our Souls

As the year begins, I want to lean into my longings, and centre in purpose. I want to know and grow my own soul.

Parts of our souls get lost and abandoned, as we endure traumas, and shape belonging around conventions and necessities.

Step 1 is a calling in, to the belonging no tyrant can take from us.

There is only one me. There is only one you.
We have singular bodies.
We are singular souls.
We belong to ourselves.
All of life, on this singular planet,
is expressed through individuality.

We belong, also, to the universe. The quantum architecture of the universe means that each unique observer stands at its centre, looking out to the edge of space and time.

Feeling into our personal centre of gravity, we find our place of belonging to the planet. We centre in time, coming home to right here and now. Can we also centre in purpose? What is your soul's calling? How can we each feel empowered to live according to our purpose? How can we deepen into belonging to ourselves?

We can cultivate gentle curiosity, and evolve capacity for tender, trustworthy care of our own souls.

FEELING MORE

Our brains' busy Default Mode Networks – with well-worn pathways of anxious rumination – help to keep us disembodied. We are lost in thought, and forever fearful of the embodied experience of our own aliveness.

Personal traumas get embedded in our tissues. Cultural prohibitions inhibit awareness of embodied feeling. Our neuroendocrine systems respond to stress by numbing body awareness. With layer upon layer of disavowal and disengagement, most of us are comfortably or uncomfortably numb.

Any simple, pleasurable practice can help us shift this. With a daily devotion to both hedonic and eudaimonic pleasures, we can train our bodies and minds to welcome more intense feelings. We can build neuroendocrine systems capable of experiencing more and more of our own embodied aliveness.

Hedonic pleasures might be as simple as savouring a meal, instead of rushing through it. We can take time to smell a baby's skin, or a fragrant flower. Listening to birdsong, or singing to the sky... by focusing on beauty, and noticing our own embodied feelings of delight, appreciation, gratitude and kindness, we build embodied neuroendocrine resource. Relishing our hedonic pleasures, we become capable of feeling more and more.

"Eudaimonic pleasure" is the joyful exhilaration of living according to our soul's purpose. There is so much pleasure, in embodied feelings of authenticity and meaning. Every time we discern and commit to what we care about, anchor in what we stand for, and take a brave step towards living as we want to live – despite the obstacles – we build embodied neuroendocrine resource. By noticing and savouring eudaimonic pleasures, we become capable of feeling more and more.

Pain practices also help us rewild our minds and build bodies capable of feeling more. Can we learn to meet sensations of pain with curiosity? After all, some people pay extra for pain! Feelings of humiliation, grief, outrage and disconnection – like body injury – create a neuroendocrine tempest within us. We can learn to stay present, as the lightning cracks and the thunder rumbles. Growing capacity to "be with" storms of embodied sensation, without immediately getting lost in thoughts about avoiding pain, we develop neuroendocrine resource. We become capable of feeling more and more.

As our bodies become capable of feeling more, they become more welcoming homes for our souls.[3]

MINDFUL EROTIC PRACTICE

We are taught that sensations of sexual arousal require immediate extinction – whether through expression or repression. Through my work as a sacred intimate, I've learned to savour sexual arousal as aliveness – and tap into a neuroendocrine well of life-giving water. Sexual arousal can empower us, for joyful and purposeful living and loving.

In a world of widespread sexual trauma and neglect, it's always vitally important to connect with sexual arousal at the pace of trust. And surely, it is equally important not to miss it. Welcoming the erotic is so very pleasurable and fruitful, and it doesn't cost a cent. Can we learn to play with walking through the world in totally turned-on bodies, alive to the beauty and sensuality around and within?

3   With thanks to Mehdi Darvish Yahya

In my own commitment to living with expanded arousal, I practice these principles:

Breath is an inner lover.

We are designed to feel sensation in the nerve-rich genital area with every single breath. Becoming aware of breathing deeply, into the pelvis, I can massage my genitals from the inside with each breath.

Why else do we walk upright?

Walking on two legs has many disadvantages. It slows us down. It makes it so much easier to get off-balance. But it puts our hands right beside our genitals! Why not enjoy the ancestors' gift?

Think of the whole body as an erogenous zone. Feel each caress.

Instead of feeling arousal only in my genitals, I want the neuroendocrine enlivenment to stream through my whole body. I imagine a full-body erection, a tingling aliveness in every cell. Wind, sun, and the branches of trees make love to me.

Give acceptance and approval to every sensation.

Instead of focusing on what I think I should feel, I want to build capacity for expanded feeling and well-being by simply noticing every sensation and emotion, with an open heart and an attitude of complete acceptance. Numbness, agitation, shame, guilt, fear, grief, boredom, and inattention can all be welcomed; they are all part of our full-spectrum aliveness.

Neuroplasticity increases with:

- intensity,
- enjoyment,
- the importance we give an activity,
- and sustained practice over time.

It feels important, for me, to schedule time to enjoy and share sexual feeling. I prioritize sex. I pay for it. I want and welcome sexual arousal into my life.

There are so many cultural prohibitions on deep embodied feeling. There are so many good reasons for people to seek soothing. Without consciously prioritizing sex, we are likely to keep it small. So many people engage in sex only in minimal, habitual, efficient ways – or not at all. Just by giving sex priority, and allocating space and time, we can tap into its resource. Expanded sexual arousal can support the rewilding of our minds, bodies and relationships, so that our souls feel cherished, and welcomed home.

MICRODOSING FOR ENCOURAGING WILD MIND

I also like to support a focus on belonging to my own soul with a multi-day microdose, using small amounts of an entheogen like LSD or psilocybin. I might try two days using a micro or mini-dose of medicine, then two days without medicine, followed by another two days with a small dose. This is usually enough to bump my thinking out of its ruts. I feel a neuroendocrine shift into a wilder mind, where I surprise myself sometimes. I am less constrained by habits and conventions.

SOUL MAPPING

"Soul Mapping" of our values and vulnerabilities is an inquiry into belonging to our souls.[4]

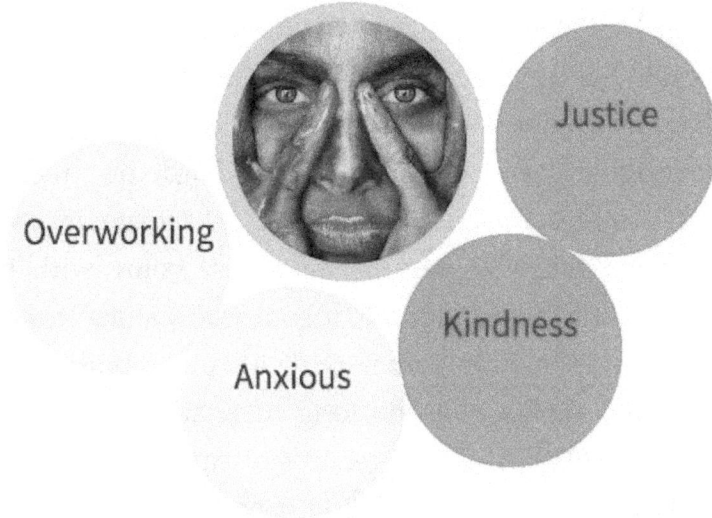

Mapping Values

Mapping values, we engage in discerning what we stand for. What are your gifts? What are you certain of? A process of reflecting on our heartfelt values supports us in becoming what we want to be. Making and renewing commitments to what we care about is an ongoing, important key to unlocking capacities for living on purpose. As we unwind embodied trauma, and learn and co-create new ways of being, we can stop navigating the world with unconscious appeasements and entitlements,

---

4   The practice of Soul Mapping emerged from studies with Wendy Baxter on Values-based Organizing and Kai Cheng Thom on Loving Justice. It builds on understandings shared in my book *Science for Sexual Happiness*.

and rules that are imposed from outside us. Our actions, words, emotions, physical presence, our level of lovingness, and what we do alone and together can increasingly match what we want to embody, and what we dream of.

Mapping Vulnerabilities

We all have ways of being that seem troublesome, to ourselves or others. We might tend to be anxious, passive, or hypervigilant. We might work too hard, or dream too small. We might habitually appease, or engage in conflict without sensitivity. Values we hold dear come with built-in vulnerabilities. For example, a soul that values loyalty in important relationships comes with a vulnerability – over-commitment can keep us too long in relationships that are harmful. A soul that values generosity can be vulnerable to resentful over-giving, and giving in ways that are unwanted.

I want us to embrace and honour our vulnerabilities – even though they might have harmful impacts. Let's always stay curious about our troublesome parts! With appreciative reflection on our vulnerabilities, we can learn to discern and honour their gifts as well as their costs. We can feel how our habitual safety shapes serve us and limit us. We can learn to hold each other's vulnerabilities as sacred, and help each other have more choice.

Sketch a Soul Map

What values do you embody? What do you like about yourself, and feel certain of? What are vulnerabilities, that need tending?

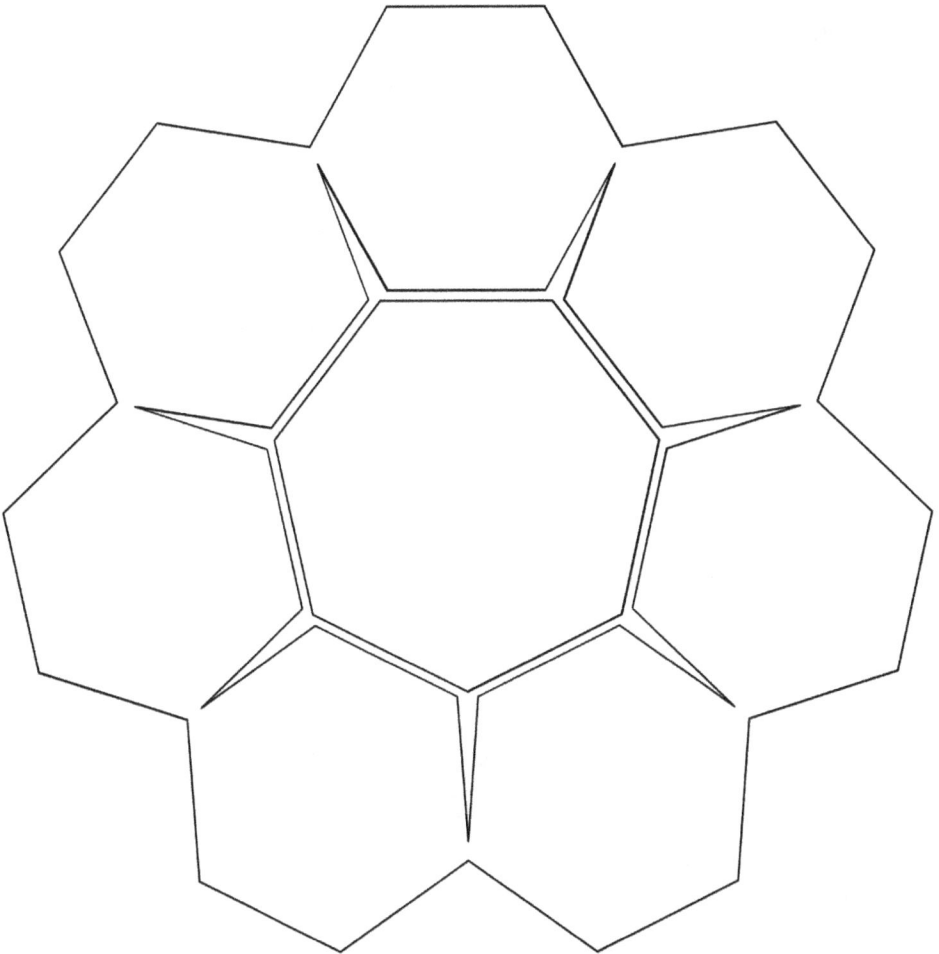

Querying and Queering the Gender Binary

Imagine being welcomed to a world that honours and celebrates your uniqueness, and supports you to feel and find it. Most of us are not. Instead we get gendered. The very first thing people say, as we are born, is, "It's a boy!" Or "It's a girl!" A whole host of social expectations and entitlements follow. We get slotted into a social system where gender – along with race, ability, class, cultural measures of intelligence and attractiveness, and other external measures – gives us relative worth. We are shaped to fit into social systems that distribute privilege and precarity, and punish every difference from an ideal norm. There are rewards for following rules and playing roles. We generate adaptive brain maps that help us hide our uniqueness. We fit in enough to survive another day. But singularity stubbornly persists. We see it in faces; we feel it in erotic responses; we know it in our souls. Our uniqueness is affirmed whenever we feel deeply loved. Committing to our own souls, and learning to feel who we are from the inside instead of judging ourselves from the outside, is a core practice-that-is-never-perfect, on this path of embodied love.

As a part of belonging to my soul, and growing more capacity to meet and cherish others' souls, I want to unwind all the ways that capitalism and colonialism shape my desires and my dreams. As one part of this inquiry, I wonder who I can become, outside of rules and roles that define gender. Who and how can I love? How do I want to express myself erotically?

There are so many factors that contribute to our experience of gender, and our gender expression. Components of gender include chromosomes, hormones, genitals, reproductive organs, personal identity, social identity, culture, environment and partner choice. Within each of these components, there are innumerable variations. Gender is an ever-emerging property of different systems that interact with each other, in ways that are everchanging. When there are so many complex contributing factors, possibilities don't just add up; they multiply. Mathematically speaking, each person's gender is unique to them.

It can be helpful to know that in fetal development, our genitals stay undifferentiated for the first seven weeks – meaning that we all have significant personal experience of life outside the gender binary. Genitals usually differentiate into some version of "innies" and "outies" depending on chromosomes, but our genitals, like our genders, are unique to us. Genitals are as different as faces, and like our faces they are ever-changing throughout our lives. It can be nice to know that vulvas have as much erectile tissue as penises, even though much of the clitoral complex is hidden beneath the skin. I encourage each person who works and plays with me to share their own names for their own unique genitals, as they learn to cherish their very own, ever-emerging truths.

Embryonic development

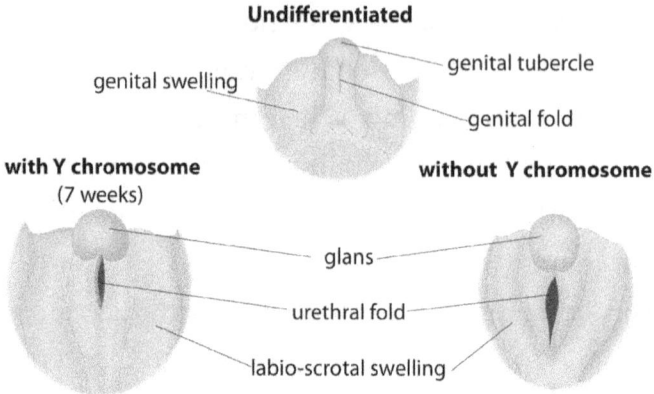

Undifferentiated

genital swelling — genital tubercle

— genital fold

with Y chromosome
(7 weeks)

without Y chromosome

glans

urethral fold

labio-scrotal swelling

Adult genitals: What do you call this?

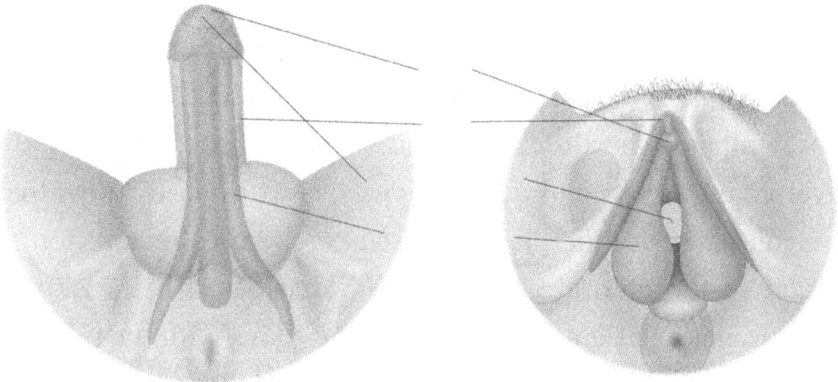

Showing homologous genital tissues in fetal development and adult genitals

Can you imagine - or remember – your soul, before gender shaped you? Is there a way to honour your gender as a quality that is unique to you? However we want to live, no matter how we love, we can take time to savour our singularity, and the uniqueness of each being in every form of life.

Queering binaries guides us to into more complex, multifaceted ways of being. We don't need to get trapped in either-or options that won't let us be fully ourselves, or fully know and love the ones we love.

Creating a Soul Retrieval Ritual

Experiences of violence, relentless microaggressions, and great griefs are everyday fare, under the regime of capitalism and colonialism. As we experience our lonely traumas, it is as if our souls leave our bodies. And it's true! The more we understand the biophysical nature of trauma's impact, the better we understand "soul loss" as an actual, embodied experience, with identifiable biophysical markers. Great dangers keep us metabolizing corrosive levels of cortisol and adrenaline. Our cells generate energy through toxic fermentation rather than sustainable cellular respiration.[5] Biorhythms get muted, so we experience less agony, but we can never fully rest. We forego ecstasy. When our bodies are carrying unprocessed trauma – or facing ongoing trauma – we might feel dissociated, loveless, listless and fragmented. We might feel restless, anxious and panicky. We might get mired in overwhelming shame, or find our minds compulsively busy with relentless blame. Unprocessed and ongoing trauma get expressed in autoimmune disorders, cardiovascular disease and inflammation. Our DNA is impacted through epigenetic markers. Traumas – large and small – have profound effects on our individual bodies and souls, and on our intimate relationships and larger communities. The experience of neglect generates biophysical effects that are similar to violent trauma.

---

5   See my book *Love and Death in a Queer Universe* for an explanation of this process, in the chapter on "Autopoesis and Failures of Love."

In my work and play as a sacred intimate, I have witnessed and participated in many hundreds of "Soul Retrieval" rituals. We can co-create sacred space and time, where our souls are invited back into our bodies. These rituals feel like watershed experiences that help us reclaim lost parts of ourselves, and become more whole. And for me, soul retrieval is not just once and done. It is an ongoing practice, and a joyful commitment. What parts of my and your soul feel lost and fragmented? How might these lost parts of us want to be welcomed home?

In a simple definition, ritual is ceremony. We participate in a planned sequence of activities, performed in a sequestered place, in a special time-outside-time. Rituals often mark a transition between one state and another, a "rite of passage," or a celebration of the sacred. In normative culture, we are often passive consumers of ritual. In the many rituals I have been part of, we are active creators.

The structure and content of a "Soul Retrieval Ritual" will be different for everyone. Some people want to create ritual alone, with the witness of trees and sky. Some want to create ritual with an intimate friend, professional ritualist, medicine guide or sacred intimate. Ritual technologies that invite a reunion of body and soul might include songs, poems, rattles, sex toys, flowers and ceremonial objects. People might include an intention to explore altered consciousness and ecstatic states, and request particular touch experiences. They might ask to hear nourishing statements that affirm and welcome their unique soul.

Soul retrieval rituals can be transformational, healing and heart-opening. And it is so important to work within our neural learning zone, so as to avoid creating an overwhelming experience that we can't integrate.

Medicine and/or erotic touch can expand our neural learning window temporarily. Under their influence, we may feel empowered to partake of experiences that exceed what our sober nervous system has capacity to integrate. Having clear discussion of our fears, desires, boundaries and limitations before any ritual feels essential. We need to ensure that our voice and choice will be accessible, and honoured, even as we enter nonordinary states of consciousness. We need to schedule time and arrange support for sufficient integration, to help us weave the meaning and magic of a Soul Retrieval ritual into our everyday world.

LISTENING TO THE "SOUL NERVE"

Resmaa Menakem usefully renames the Vagus Nerve as the "Soul Nerve." He describes how this "highly complex and extraordinarily sensitive organ … communicates through vibes and sensations" within and between us.[6]

6   *My Grandmother's Hands*, p. 138

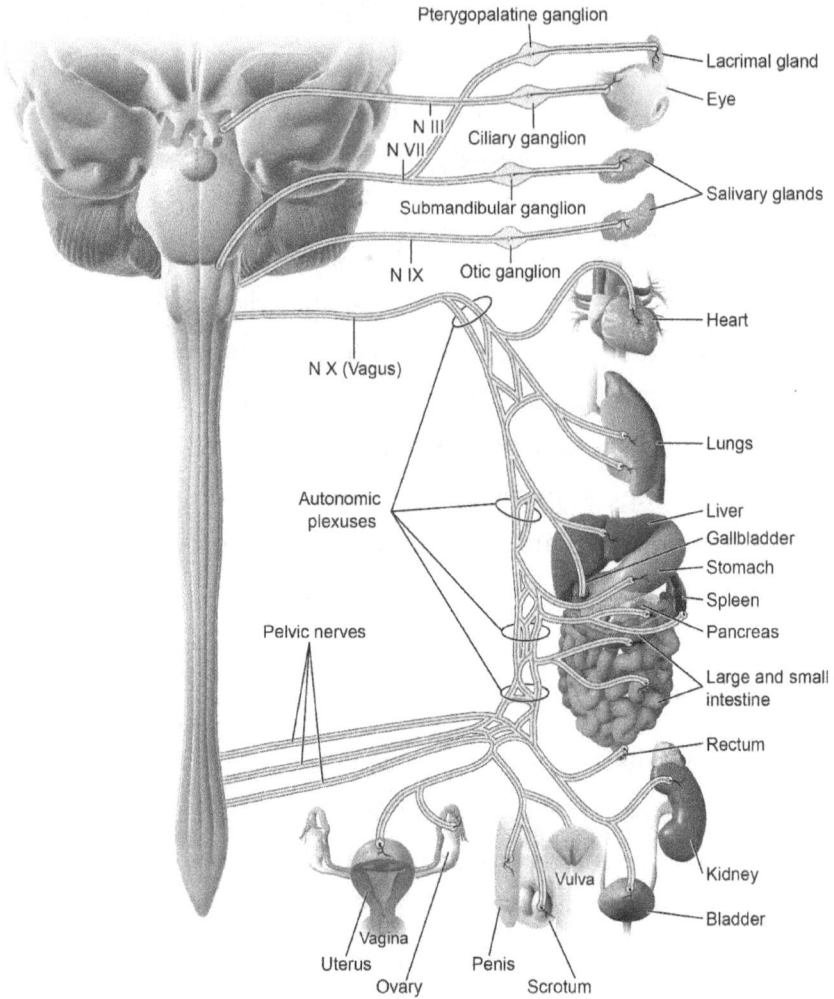

Parasympathetic innervation, showing the vagus nerve.
drawing by Blausen.com staff, Blausen gallery 2014 with edits by Caffyn Jesse

Moving courageously, at the pace of trust, as we attend to vibes and sensations, we can use embodied practices of breath, sound, movement, imagination and touch to soothe and excite our soul nerves, inviting our souls into our bodies and relationships. As Menakem guides, embodied practices are foundational to creating bodies and relationships with capacity to practice antiracism, and courageously resist the hegemony of white-body supremacy. Without actual embodied practices, we stay ruled by fear. White people will keep using their privilege to escape and externalize danger, perpetuating trauma in the name of safety. People powered by trauma-induced dissociation, shame and blame will keep on threatening to annihilate the biosphere.

As we try to co-create conditions where Soul Retrieval becomes possible, we want to enter a resonant field, where bodies, minds, spirits and emotions feel aligned. To find our way to resonance, we need to attend the vibrations and sensations of our soul nerves. We need embodied practices that support us in growing Vagal Fitness, as we listen to our own bodies and to other bodies. We need awareness of our personal and interpersonal "Neural Learning Zone," so we can notice when it feels to be safe-enough-to-be-brave. We can't magically transcend oppressions and privileges, and our practiced patterns of appeasement and unconscious entitlements. Soul Retrieval requires our patient learning, and sustained, embodied love.

MARCH AND APRIL: BELONGING TO EACH OTHER

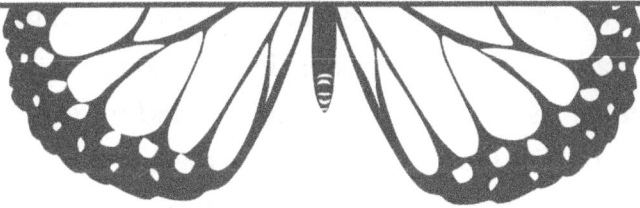

I belong to those I love.

*I practice welcoming and cherishing them,
including their unlovable parts.*

The Relational Matrix

In March and April, with Spring unfolding its magic all around me, I like to focus on belonging to those I love. By deepening into "Belonging to Each Other," we can ignite our wild imaginations and daring dreams.

Everywhere in the wild world, there are guides to better belonging. As a river belongs to a valley, as a flower belongs to a bee... we can belong to a web of love, wherein the whole is greater than the sum of its parts. A valley gets carved into being by a river; a river comes to exist by being held in a valley's embrace. Flowers and pollinators co-evolve in ways that are ever-changing. We can belong to the reciprocal co-creation that is ever-emerging. In the intimate, intricate weave of each particular us, I am empowered to become more fully me. When we are cherished as our singular selves in enduring intimacies, we can better burrow through traumatic acculturation, and find our way home to who we want to go on becoming.

I am forever coming into being in a relational matrix. There are intimate friends, and chosen family. And there is the web of culture and community. Who are the poets and teachers that inspire? What are the groups where I feel belonging? Particular ecosystems, plants and animals also hold me and guide me, in my ever-emergent process of being and becoming.

There are necessary discernments, in this process. The birds guide and inspire, as every morning, at this time of year, they sing, to call in partnerships, and celebrate survival. They listen for each other. With exquisitely sensitive hearing, they weave a symphony of sound... even though there is always another kind of noise vibrating through the air. There's a loud buzz of traffic from a nearby road. Airplanes fly overhead; there are distant chainsaws. But birds discern. Somehow, they ignore the noise, and listen to the music. They belong to the song.

I want to be like birds, as I attune to my web of belonging, both human and non-human. Can I listen for the sweet music of each person I love, without getting distracted by all the noise? Can we keep on discerning the song only we can sing, in the weave of each particular us? What if I give my attention to the music, with more and more precision? How can I belong to the song?

One of my friends is like a mountain where the swirling dust of me can come to rest, and deepen into being soil. Another friend is a rooted willow, holding my swamp and slime, so the muddy waters of me have a place to clarify. Another love of mine is like a hummingbird, sipping the sweet nectar of me, so I yearn to deepen in colour, and vulnerably open....

BELONGING TO EACH OTHER

What can loving relationship be?

How good can it get?

Capitalism and colonialism describe people as replaceable and disposable. If we aren't serving a purpose, we get tossed. If we break the rules, we get incarcerated, disciplined and punished. Everyone feels alone and afraid. We try to deny, hide, fix and change those parts of ourselves and each other that don't meet expectations, follow rules or play roles. Making mistakes makes us into mistakes; we are filled with shame and blame. If we don't fight back against the relationship paradigms of the dominant culture, our intimate lives can feel like barren deserts, or bloody battlegrounds.

How do we find the people we belong to, and commit to love? People have ways of being so unlovable! When their unlovable parts trigger our unlovable parts, we fight or fume. We want something so much better! We resign ourselves to settling for less, or we look for an exit. Step 2 is a calling in to the patient, imperfect practice of lasting, loving relationship. We can fail each other, and disappoint ourselves, and still reach for more and better love. There are medicines and practices to guide us.

Trustworthy relationships are where I feel empowered to unfold self-trust; my capacity for loving relationships is amplified simultaneously. The web of open-hearted love we make can spiral out to touch the world around us, while it spirals in to hold us evermore intimately. I cannot be me without our love.

An important aspect of enduring love is growing our willingness to embrace the agony of unwanted change. We fail each other, disappoint each other, and stop wanting each other in the same ways. We have unmet needs and harmful impacts. Sometimes we need separation, distance and ends. Can we still choose love?

I share here some "Belonging to Each Other" practices that have helped me co-create lasting, loving relationships that consistently thrill me. Relationship Mapping feels foundational. I want to feel myself embedded in a web of relationships I am committed to. The "Welcome Home" ritual – and an overall orientation to welcoming all our parts, including those that are hard to hold – have become primary resources in all my relations. Trauma-aware touch is a practice that cultivates lovingness. We thrive in the biophysical experience of embodied love.

Empathogens like MDMA are potent medicines that can help us rewire neuroendocrine defaults; they can resource joyful, enduring intimacies.

Before we begin experimenting with any of these embodied practices, we need to find our way to people who feel safe enough and brave enough to practice with. If we have not found our people yet, we can practice in our imaginations. Imagining doing these exercises will generate biophysical changes and shift our inner neuroendocrine environment. We can each begin to change our own biomagnetic field, so we better attract what we want, and protect against what we don't want.

When we have experienced harmful relationships, we often become skilled at avoiding belonging to others, in various ways. We can be simultaneously hypervigilant to insult and injury, and able to ignore and deny truly dangerous relationship dynamics. Through both hypervigilance and dissociation, we experience dangerous others, and learn to trust people less and less.

In safe-enough, brave-enough relationships, we experience the respect, connection and care we need to support the settling of our physiology. When we feel cherished, and also challenged in manageable ways, we experience a cascade of beneficial physiological effects.

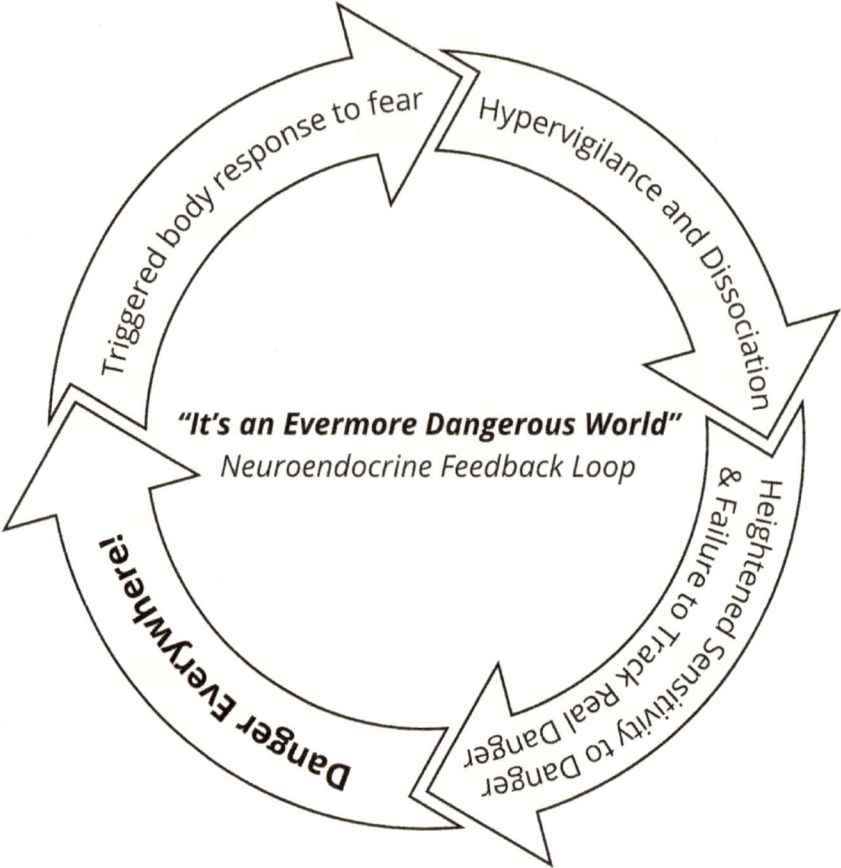

"It's an Evermore Dangerous World"
Neuroendocrine Feedback Loop

Triggered body response to fear

Hypervigilance and Dissociation

Heightened Sensitivity to Danger & Failure to Track Real Danger

Danger Everywhere!

These graphics show how neuroendocrine feedback loops get established in our bodies and relationships. Our personal and interpersonal neurobiology can either contribute to an evermore dangerous world, or an evermore wonderful world. And there is more.... With ecstatic practice, we can navigate and co-create a miraculous world, see graphic on page 60.

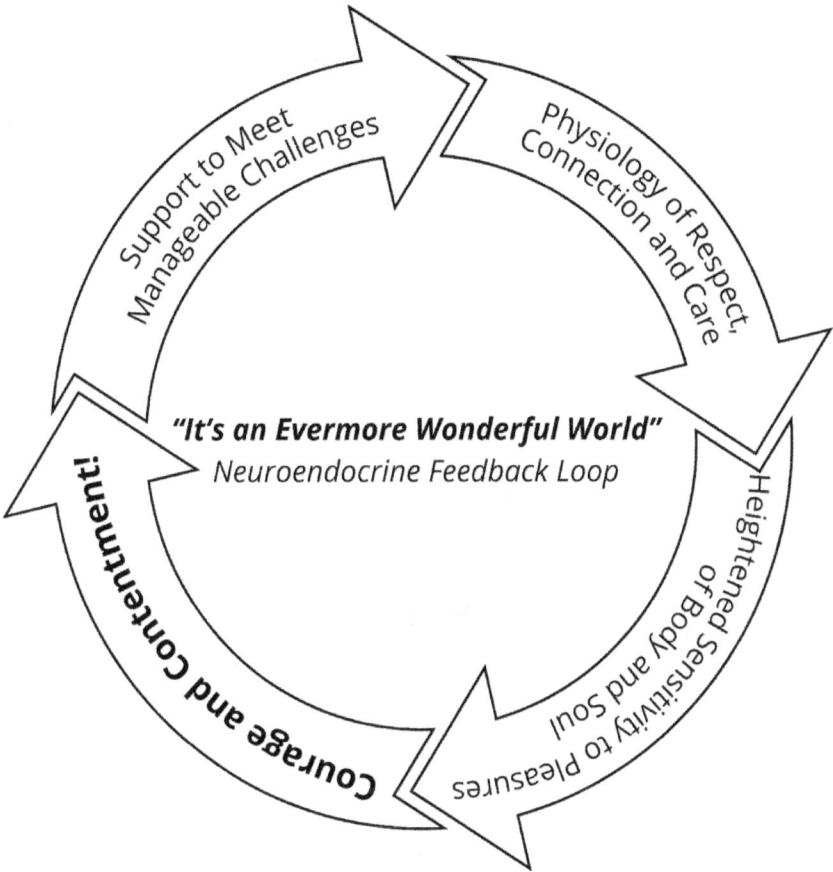

"It's an Evermore Wonderful World"
Neuroendocrine Feedback Loop

Support to Meet Manageable Challenges

Physiology of Respect, Connection and Care,

Heightened Sensitivity to Pleasures of Body and Soul

Courage and Contentment!

RELATIONSHIP MAPPING

Mapping and tracking people who support us in living our soul's purpose, we anchor ourselves in a matrix of trustworthy relationships. Mapping helps us discern.[7]

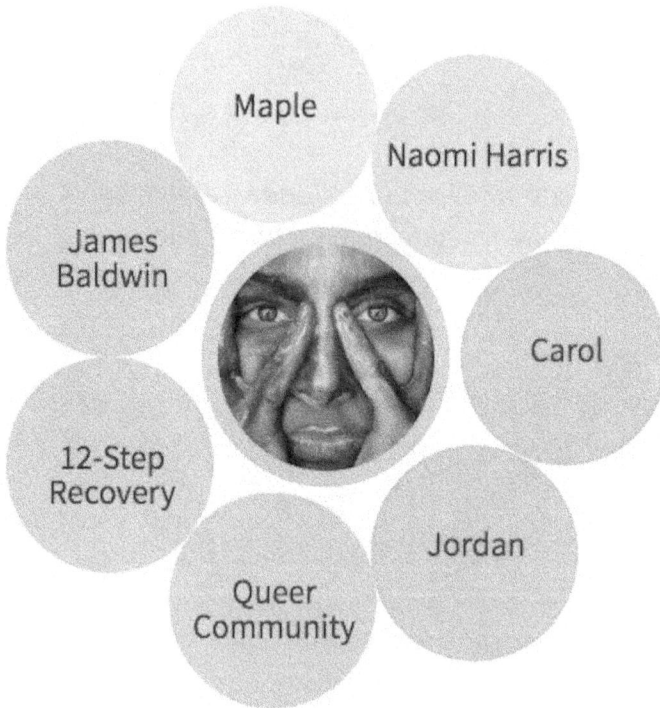

Who helps us be who we want to be?

Who can hold us in the process of making mistakes and learning from them?

Who can honour our most powerful – and paltry – feelings, while they affirm and anchor us in belonging to what we care about?

7   Based on Pod Mapping by Mia Mingus.

Maps orient us as we explore new worlds. With reassurance and support from trustworthy friends, mentors, and communities of practice, we can ground in the values we want to embody, even in a crisis. We can better take courageous action to repair, when we have done harm, and know when to engage in or avoid conflict. We can live guided by what we value, and be cherished and supported in our vulnerabilities. Mapping relationships can feel very vulnerable. We may realize we are more isolated than we thought, or more connected – or often, a little of both!

Sketch a Relationship Map

Who are the intimate allies who know and cherish you? Who can support you in learning from mistakes? Who do you want to build relationship with? What groups and teachings help you be who you want to be?

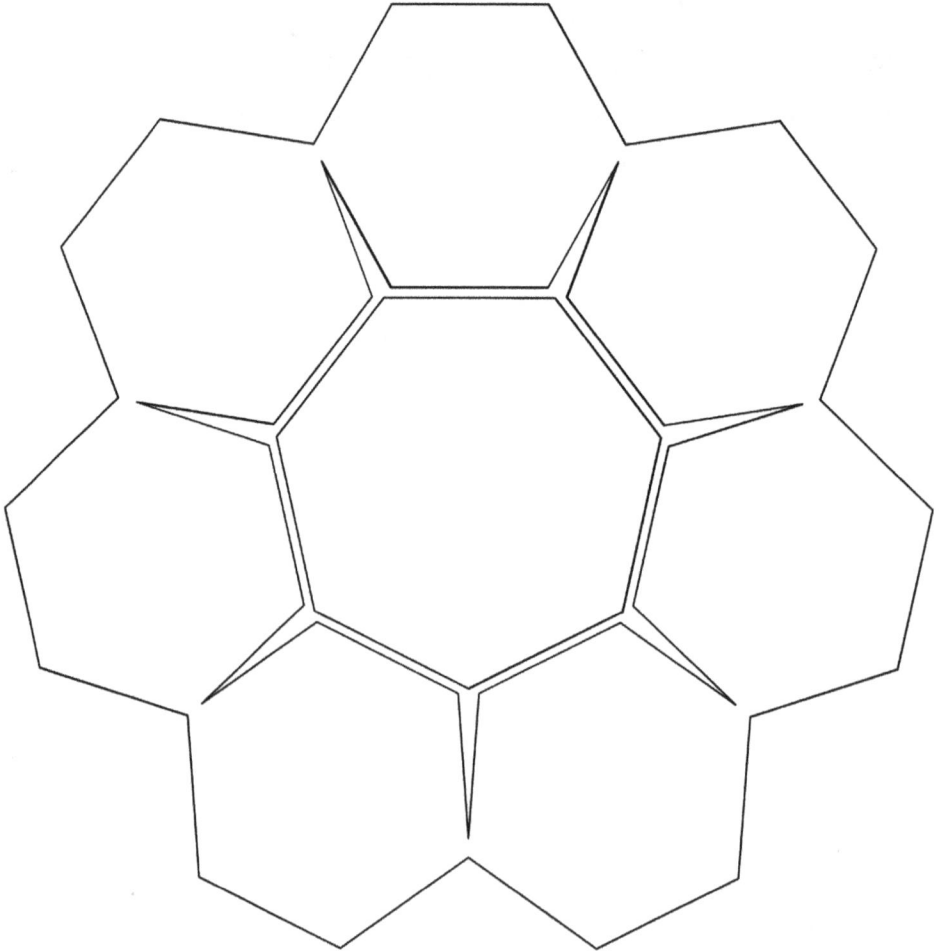

WELCOME HOME RITUAL

A Welcome Home ritual[8] creates space, time and loving support for welcoming and integrating any aspect of ourselves that feels hard to hold. It may be some part of us that feels ugly, shameful and unlovable – a part we have tried hard to fix or change. Unlovable parts I have had welcomed home include these parts I have given names to:

- How Dare you? (contempt, outrage)
- Collapsed Mineshaft (impossible grief)
- Be-the-One (self-importance)
- Hide-away (fearful, lying)
- My Best is Not Good Enough (failure, incapacity)

A Welcome Home ritual can also be an exploration of a part that's felt too wonderful, big, bold and accomplished to have welcomed. Perhaps some new part of you is emerging, in a different experience of sex, gender or relationship. Or perhaps life is bringing you new experiences and identities to integrate. When it was time for me to retire as a teacher of somatic sex education, a recognition of my incompetence struggled to emerge. I was lovingly held in this uncomfortable process by dear comrades, in a Welcome Home ritual that supported my recognition to exist, and be transformed into guidance for a new way of being. (There's a video of this process included in Module 5 of my Intimacy Educator program.)

In a Welcome Home ritual, we take turns supporting each other in staying with the discomfort, rather than soothing it. As we tentatively articulate how we embody this part, we are held

---

8   This practice was developed with dear friends Tricia Bowler and Michael Haines. They teach a version of this in their "Grace of Existence" program. See their website at BeingHeld.ca

by our companions' caring touch, non-invasive curiosity, and commitment to welcome emerging and diverging truths. With support, we can grow awareness of stressful feelings without having to soothe them. We can take time to notice the shape, density, vibration, movement impulse, age and impact of a new or unwanted part of ourselves, without trying to make the sensations of discomfort stop or change. We notice nuance. We begin to understand contradictory aspects of this part of us. We gain insight into why this part exists and persists, or why it is wanting to emerge. We notice its gifts. In harvesting a ritual experience, we often feel how we can embody a hitherto unwanted part of ourselves with more excitement and peace, going forward.

Sharing these rituals with trustworthy friends over time, we feel our awful, secret parts held and welcomed. Our journeys and insights relate and integrate with each other. We begin to feel loved by other humans as we really are, instead of how others wish we were, or how we want to be. Doing these rituals regularly, we make a place where we don't need to forge belonging by denying parts of ourselves, or outlawing people we've judged to be bad and wrong. We can better feel how all our parts are loveable, even though they may sometimes have harmful impacts. We can better see and be accountable for unintended harm, when we accept and integrate the motivations, achievements and wily ways of our problematic parts.

Welcome Home can be an occasional, transformative ritual. It can also be an everyday practice. When we meet a part of ourselves or others that we don't like, can we stay curious? Can we orient to welcoming, instead of going into fixing, shame and blame, in our ordinary conversations and community life?

As the welcomer(s):

- Ask questions that support the person's inner teacher emerging, rather than offering them negative or positive judgments, reassurance or solutions.
- Repeat language used by the person being held, rather than bringing in your own words to describe this part.
- Affirm and welcome the part being held. Honour its superpowers.

STEM QUESTIONS

- Where is this part in your body? What does it feel like? Does it have a colour/density/shape/vibration?
- If this part wanted to move, how would it move?
- If this part had a voice, what would it say?
- How old is this part? Is there a story about this part, that wants to be shared?
- How has this part protected you? How has it been a gift to you/to others?
- How would this part like to be touched? How would it feel even more welcomed?

Affirmations

- I want to learn from this part of you.
- This part is so welcome.
- I honour the superpowers of this part.

As the one whose part is being welcomed:

- Take quiet time within the ritual. Keep deepening into feeling yourself.
- Let your companions' questions land, taking time to feel the impact in your body.
- Let your words and stories emerge from non-ordinary consciousness, rather than offering insights you've already had, or telling stories you already know.
- Request touch that helps you hold in your uncomfortable feelings, rather than soothing them prematurely.

TRAUMA-AWARE TOUCH

We all get lots of experience enduring unwanted touch. Neglect and violence are both ubiquitous. We need practice and support, to be able to really tune into our desires, and voice them. We need to be able to examine expectations and address unconscious entitlements, so we can hear one another's requests, without experiencing desires as demands. As we co-create a relational matrix to heal relational wounding, we need space and support enough to know ourselves, and understand how we can offer focused loving presence to another.

We can heal and resource our nervous systems with pleasurable, wanted touch. Touch can be explored in ways that please our souls and coax them home into our bodies. But in the wake of trauma and neglect, it's hard to choose physical and relational pleasure while staying in our neural learning zones. It's so important not to experience too much, too fast – and equally important not to settle for too little, too long.

For those who want to go deeper into how to offer trauma-aware, whole-body touch, I offer an extensive online course on the art and science of sacred intimacy. But here I can reduce all I ever learned and taught into a single sentence: "Touch with love." When you touch someone, know that you are touching their entire history, their deepest wounds, their secret identity, their healing powers and their most profound capacities for joy. Touch each person in their woundedness and their wonderfulness. Touch the suffocating encasement of their ordinariness. Touch it all with love. For all the tools, toys, exercises and techniques I teach and recommend, love is the only act or attitude I think is essential.

Love, in the way I mean here, has nothing to do with standards of attractiveness, partner choice, or making the selective judgments that usually limit what we call love. I exchange touch with people who are old and young, fat and thin, conventionally attractive and not. I offer loving touch to strangers – people I have never seen before and will never see again. I explore ecstasies with men, women, and those of us who are both or neither. Each time, with every person I touch, my passion – my vocation – is to love.

This love is not an abstract concept or an empty word. It is a biophysical experience that emerges through our patient, brave, kind embodied practice.

With tender, exciting whole-body touch, we love each other's bodies, impacting neurochemistry and endocrine function. Honouring toes, ears, scars and thighs, we touch the personal histories embedded in our cells. We contradict self-loathing, soothe the effects of trauma, and replace the imprints of painful, unwanted touch with pleasurable, respectful touch.

We love each other's minds, as we coax communication, and honour each person in their desires, while honouring our own boundaries. We listen to each person's stories with unconditional positive regard, inviting new neural pathways linking brain with voice and feeling. We love each other's spirits. I feel my own spirit soar, as I greet yours with wonder and amazement. We connect emotionally, and offer love as one wounded human being to another. Riding waves of emotion, we travel from deep grief to elation in a single session. This is love in action. All the other tools and techniques I teach help us co-create a counternormative framework, so we can come together in the imperfect practice of embodied love. All the exercises and understandings I have taught and invented help us connect with each other, and ourselves, for long enough so love can do its work. Embodied love is what supports me becoming the singular one that only I can be, in love with the singular one of you.

The world of normative belonging is so unloving. Love that really wants and welcomes us – love that can really feel and find us – is rare and precious. The singularity each one of us is goes on emerging, in a relational matrix where we consistently, kindly and generously offer each other trauma-aware touch and embodied love.

If you want more resources on sharing embodied love with others, as a way of life or livelihood, see my online program *Intimacy Educator*.

LEARNING AND UNLEARNING WITH EMPATHOGENS

MDMA is a potent nervous system stimulant that enhances our empathic connection and sense of belonging to others. The drug generates a flood of magnocellular oxytocin and reopens a neural learning window for social belonging – a window that otherwise closes in late adolescence. Instead of being stuck with the messages about belonging that we learned in our teens, we can go on learning.

The neurochemical signalling mechanisms that guide our feelings of belonging are ancient, and they are conserved across species and through every form of life. Research shows that octopuses – predominantly asocial and solitary animals for hundreds of millions of years – long for belonging when they ingest MDMA![9]

I have found that the occasional, ritual use of MDMA (or a related empathogen such as 3MMC) can be an empowering resource in enduring intimacies. Creating regular ritual time with those we love – with or without the support of an empathogen – can support us in choosing our love for each other, again and again.

9   Edsinger E. and Dölen G. A

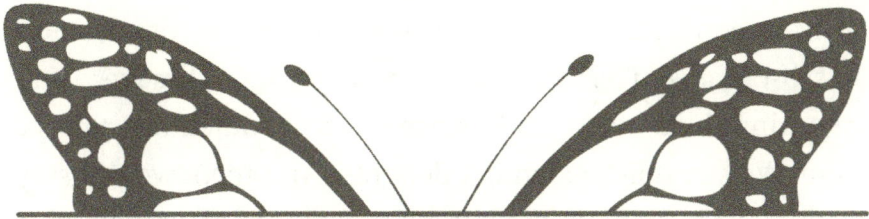

MAY AND JUNE:
BELONGING TO ECSTASY

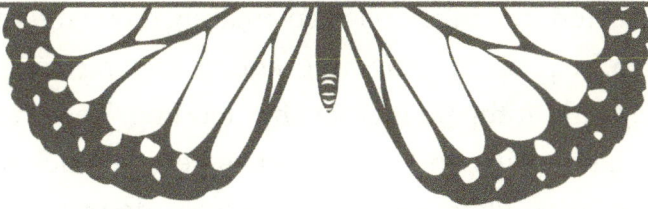

I want ecstasy.

I commit to belonging to my longing.

ECSTASY AND EQUILIBRIUM

As the days grow longer and longer, in May and June, every growing thing vibrates with aliveness. I feel inspired. Reaching for ecstatic dimensions of my living, as you reach for yours, and we reach together for ecstatic connection between us, we travel a path that takes us far, far from equilibrium – and it is a path that aligns us with every living thing, and with the interconnected nonequilibrium systems of the biosphere. As far from equilibrium as we can travel, we enter climax states of self-organized criticality. By noticing our climaxes, and savouring them, we open to surprises that sometimes emerge there. We can relish extended delights. And then, we can stay conscious throughout the cascade of extended orgasm that takes us back to equilibrium. Then we can rest in satisfaction – enjoying the peace and the bliss.

Finding a generative, joyful relationship between ecstasy and equilibrium can guide us in co-creating erotic interactions. It can also help us in imagining and practicing community organizing, and intimate relationship tending. Too often I see people, relationships and communities getting stuck in over-attachment to equilibrium. Safety feels so desirable; anxiety makes us tremulous. We fear the instability of non-equilibrium systems, and we live in a culture that doesn't guide our fear into finding a courageous reach for ecstasy.

In equilibrium-driven systems, all change becomes balanced. Over time, net change is zero. Things stay the same. In non-equilibrium systems, balance is broken. Over time, a non-zero value emerges. Things change. When interconnected systems far from equilibrium emerge, entropy decreases, and can sometimes even be reversed. All of life is a non-equilibrium system.

Capitalism and colonialism have taught us to distrust ecstasy. We are trained to hide and minimize our ecstasies, and to regulate, monetize and privatize them. We ascribe them to gurus, or special substances, things we can buy, or particular lovers. We don't notice subtle climax states within and around us. We ignore our orgasms. But we can reclaim ecstasy. It is part of our integrity. It can resource and support all our intimacies. It can bring us into right relationship with equilibrium.

Ecstatic practices are part of every ancient and indigenous human culture. Western culture keeps us separated from each other and our own capacities. We endure the overwhelm of lonely traumas, then spend the rest of our lives trying to calm our nervous systems – breathing less, shutting down our lusts and longings, and soothing ourselves with food, alcohol, shopping…. There are so many soothing practices, and so many good reasons to want soothing. Often, soothing is an excellent choice that keeps us alive for another day. But if we never find our way to the places and people that support our stretch into courageous engagement, then our injured souls stay small. We don't belong to our longings. We actively inhibit ecstasy.

Ecstatic Practices

Breath

Sweats

Body Mortification

Fasting

Rites of Passage

Drumming

Chanting

Erotic Practices

Collective Joy Practices

Collective Grief Practices

Psychedelic Medicine

Ecstatic practices can be as simple as breathing more, masturbating longer or eating less. Cold water swimming, getting a tattoo, participating in a demonstration, or engaging in hours of lovemaking, we exit equilibrium. We challenge our neuroendocrine systems as we reach for more. Choosing ecstatic practice is not so simple, for those of us raised without training and cultural support. Rites of passage, and regular, embodied experiences of ecstasy are needed, if we want to keep on stretching into our discomforts courageously. Personal and collective joy and grief practices keep us anchored in the rhythms of ecstasy.

ORGASMS

We are reliably guided by our longing for more and better ecstasies, so long as we pay attention to our orgasms. Orgasms happen along the outer edge of ecstasy, when we are critically far from equilibrium. Through orgasm, we exit highly excited, unstable states and come into the equilibrium of peaceful satisfaction. Orgasms can be subtle and small, or monumental, earth-shaking cascades.

People often come to work with a sacred intimate because they aren't satisfied with their orgasms. They want orgasms that are bigger, better, more accessible, less uncontrolled. They want the orgasms they see in porn. They don't want their orgasms wired to specific fantasies or practices. My loving answer to all the different longings is – let's reorient away from external goalposts, and all the rules and roles that come from outside us. Let's take time to notice what's happening within us. Let's get familiar with the orgasms we are already experiencing, and learn to welcome them, and pay attention.

How many ways – and how many times of day – do we experience climax states? When and how does energy expand, peak, and then release? How do we feel peace in the afterglow? What's going on in your body, mind, spirit and emotions, as you savour? By paying attention to all the ways we climax, and learning to linger in many forms of satisfaction, people can become more and more capable of knowing and growing their very own version of orgasmic life. We can keep feeling and finding moments of ecstatic belonging, in which we savour abundance, and feel connection.

To practice noticing every arc of arousal, we need to learn to stay present with sensations of discomfort and agitation, without prematurely seeking soothing. It helps to have companions who don't want us to stop feeling, but who can accept and honour numbness, when that's what's there for us. If we keep tracking our cells and our souls, we'll keep growing more and more capacity for excited arousal, in various ways. We can start noticing many little orgasmic cascades that happen, throughout the day. Let's take time to celebrate and savour!

Every time that neuroendocrine arousal climaxes, we can come to rest in a refractory period. Biophysically, and relationally, satisfaction is an endless well of ongoing emergence. When there is a reference point for our excitements, and a resting point, desires can get more courageous. Savouring satisfactions is a practice that resources us – so we can better lean into our longings. If we notice our satisfactions, we'll find our way to more satisfactions, then more and more.

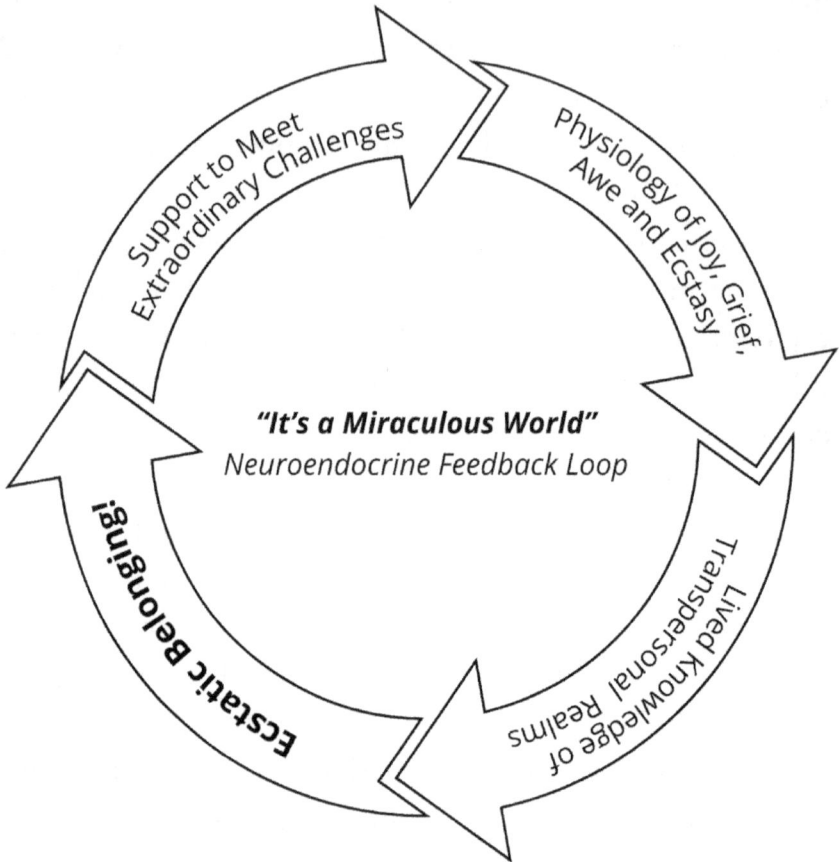

Ecstatic practices set up a feedback loop in our personal and interpersonal neurobiology. We can grow a miraculous world, within and between us.

WHEN PLEASURE AND ORGASM ARE INACCESSIBLE

"Anorgasmia" is a medical diagnosis that pathologises infrequent or absent orgasms – or less-intense orgasms. "Anhedonia" is a diagnosis that pathologises people's inability to feel pleasure – a common symptom of depression. For me, anorgasmia and anhedonia are not pathologies. They are wise ways our bodies find to attach to equilibrium, and anchor in a feeling of union and communion with all life.

Pleasure-seeking systems drive us away from belonging. They ask that we want something for our singular selves, and honour our appetites. That is why "Belonging to Ecstasy" is Step 3, and it needs to be preceded by Step 1 ("Belonging to Our Souls") and Step 2 ("Belonging to Each Other"). If we are resourced by embodied experiences of belonging to our singular selves, *and* we feel belonging in a web of loving relationship, we can better belong to our own longings as they drive us – temporarily – away from belonging.

We find our way to "ecstatic belonging" through first amplifying, then exceeding, our singular selves. Orgasm brings us into the experience of a transpersonal unity with all life. In the regime of capitalism and colonialism, we get more practice feeling "traumatic belonging." We belong partially, provisionally, by keeping ourselves small. We constrain ourselves, and truncate our longings. We struggle against violence, until we flatline through despair. In the dissociative self-abandonment of trauma, we abandon hope, and surrender agency. Self-awareness is extinguished through the dorsal-vagal drop of deep dissociation.

For people without developed capacity for ecstasy, the reach for orgasm can feel profoundly unsafe. Orgasm can trigger body memories of dissociative self-abandonment. With patient practice, working in our own personal and interpersonal neural learning zones, we can start to distinguish our neuroendocrine capacity for joyful self-leaving, through transpersonal experiences of ecstatic belonging, from the self-abandonment triggered by trauma. In time, I do think it's important to weave these experiences together, in experiencing a full-spectrum neuroendocrine system. This is discussed in the chapter on "Belonging to Non-Being."

When people can't access orgasm, they are often not attending subtle orgasmic sensations that keep flattening their arousal out of uncomfortable non-equilibrium states. By paying attention to the arc of arousal, and savouring mini-orgasms, we can learn to welcome and tolerate increasing arousal, access more experiences of climax, and savour more of the peace, equilibrium, and ongoing emergence, in orgasm's afterglow.

Many conscious experiences of noticing how orgasm is such a trustworthy guide of non-equilibrium states might help us navigate the frightening, far-from-equilibrium states of the social sphere, the biosphere, and our own intimate spheres. As we co-create new (or ancient) culture that wants and values ecstasy, and resource ourselves with regular ecstatic practice, we are building biophysical capacities for navigating the unprecedented dangers of these times.

Erotic Practice: Notice and Cultivate Orgasms

An orgasm can be experienced as a simple reflex response, like an involuntary genital sneeze – announcing of the limits of non-equilibrium that a body can tolerate. (Hence orgasm sometimes occurs during the horror of sexual assault.) Alternatively, orgasm can be experienced as an ecstatic alchemy, soulful and transcendent. I don't privilege my spiritual experiences of expanded orgasms over simple reflex responses. All the ways I orgasm are welcome, and can be productively noticed and savoured.

We can consciously access amplified experiences of orgasm, and explore multiple orgasms, by tuning in to technologies of full embodiment. Breath, sound, movement, imagination and touch can be used to stimulate various aspects of the nervous system that contribute to arousal and orgasm, and help us better integrate their functioning. Savouring all our orgasms, and spending time in postorgasmic bliss, are keys to changing our neuroendocrine systems, and building capacity to embody more and more ecstasy.

For those who want more specific guidance and support, I have many books, online courses and free videos that you can access through my website. There are many exercises – ranging from breath practices through extended genital massage – that we can use to cultivate more frequent orgasmic experiences, and to enjoy their infinite variety.

ECSTATIC RITUAL EXPERIENCE

For me, ecstasy is an everyday practice. In addition, when I am consciously focusing on this step, I like to create a larger "Rite of Passage" – a ritual ecstatic experience. Intention for transformation, and commitment to harvesting and integration, are key to creating this kind of ritual.

We can invite the ecstasy of exceeding of our singular selves through a psychedelic medicine experience, an Ecstatic Erotic Massage ritual, or some other ecstatic practice. In accessing an ecstatic experience of psychedelic medicine, I want to work with a trustworthy guide who can tend my physical safety, and support me emotionally as I journey with a larger dose of psychedelic medicine. If I am reaching for expanded ecstatic states in an erotic ritual, then I want a dedicated time experiencing full-body touch without having to be concerned about a partner's pleasure.

To cultivate my neuroendocrine capacity for more ecstasy, with an Erotic Ritual, I use breathing patterns that amplify my arousal (with more oxygen), and calm my body enough to stay with amplified arousal (with less oxygen). I keep a vibrator handy, to be sure I can access multiple orgasms. I co-create these rituals with trustworthy friends.

I imagine that by sharing a wide variety of ecstatic rituals, and inspiring each other, we can co-create culture that values and cultivates ecstasy.

In the communities of practice I celebrate and invite, we find expanded safety and peace through nurturing what is brave. I don't want to stay safe. I want space and time to practice feeling fear, without reaching prematurely for soothing. Fear transforms into courage, when it is held in embodied love.

Blending Erotic Friendship with Psychedelic Medicines

I hosted a retreat in my home in 2023 to explore the intersections of empowered choice and voice, whole-body touch, erotic friendship and psychedelic medicines. A small group of great souls came together. We all arrived as experienced spaceholders – courageous and seasoned explorers of expanded dimensions of our personal and interpersonal neuroendocrine systems. We had all done much work with our personal traumas and triggers. We all already knew how to delight in difference, and tend to rupture with repair. We all were already oriented by our own trustworthy longings – for deep pleasure, and profound ecstasy. And every resource we had grown within us was needed for this inquiry.

We made a unique blend of lovership and leadership – in this gathering that had never been before and will never be again. And something extraordinary emerged. The molecules conspired. The rhythm of the biosphere found expression in hearts, breath, imagination and co-creation. Death and life made love within and around us, as they do in forest, soil, cells, souls, skin…. We found a path of ever-deepening differentiation within evermore unity. We each and all could shine, and reflect each other's shining. Extraordinary experiences got woven with everyday frustrations, trauma triggers and ongoing commitment to care. As I reflected and rested, in the weeks following the retreat, I felt resourced by many embodied experiences of life as it is meant to be. I found myself incubating mysterious new dreams.

For me, Eros is our sacred well, our inmost core. Psychedelics weave us into conscious connection with the web of life and death; we feel wanted and welcome. And so the intersection of somatic sexual wellness with psychedelic medicines can be a place of powerful magic – but also of grave danger, and potential for major misattunements. Combining them is not for the under-resourced, inexperienced, or faint-of-heart. If this is a weave that calls to you, I hope you go carefully, finding your very own pace of trust, with those great souls who are your precious companions. I'd love to learn what you discover. Because I'm going to stay, and work and play at this intersection. It is messy, challenging, and full of mystery. And it also feels profoundly right.

JULY AND AUGUST:
BELONGING TO INTERBEING

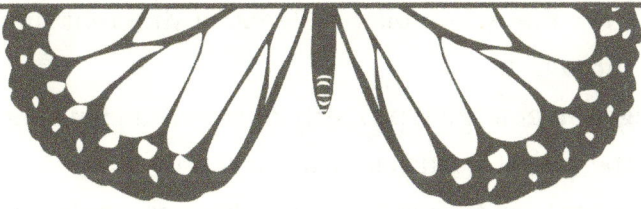

*I belong to the biosphere
that lives through me.*

A GLOBAL CONSPIRACY

Interbeing is everywhere, but we have been taught not to notice.[10] To be is to inter-be, in sacred partnership with all that is other. July and August are months I want to be outdoors, swimming naked, sleeping under stars, experiencing interbeing in my cells and skin.

Western culture gaslights us with stories of independent individualities. We learn to fear and deny our interdependence. We almost believe the story that we are meant to maximize "self-interest" by dominating and controlling all that is other. Can we create space and time, within and between us, to live into a different story? We can begin by noticing how we exist as interdependent beings and processes. Each human being is the stardust we are made of; we are the earth, air, fire and water. We are the plants and animals we eat; we are the microorganisms, rain and soil our molecules become and come from. We are many complex systems, at different timescales, that live through us.

Being is an emergent property of interbeing, at every level. Quarks, the tiniest particles of matter, only exist in hadrons, where they matter to one another. Lithosphere, hydrosphere and atmosphere conspire to co-create a biosphere. Fungi, plants and animals come into being through a web of love. The 100 trillion cells that comprise each one of us exist in symbiotic partnership with the 100 trillion separate beings of our microbiome. We are one with the planet's intricate network of molecules; our interlinked individualities are ever-emergent truths. Focusing on interbeing means inviting the sacred

10 *The term Interbeing was coined and beautifully explained by Thich Nhat Hanh*

partnerships we are made of, and made for, to be known by our souls, and to inform our intimacies and communities.

We are a global conspiracy of interbeing. Etymologically, conspiracy means to breathe together; we con-spire. Together, we manifest the miraculous. According to the laws of physics, the biosphere should not exist. Deepening our allegiance to interbeing, we join as one with this impossible, counternormative planet. With stars and ancestors, in the web of life and death, we can listen and share stories. Like Shahrazad in the story of "1001 nights," we can make our stories so beautiful and full of intrigue, that we win life together for one more night. It can be a night of deep delight. In my very being, I want to be a commitment to the global conspiracy of interbeing.

CULTIVATING SURRENDER WITH BREATH, SEX AND ENTHEOGENS

In my embodied experience of Belonging to Ecstasy, I go through an amplification of my individuality, then I exceed it, to arrive at a transpersonal experience of post-orgasmic bliss. Through excited arousal, I access belonging through the sympathetic branch of my nervous system. In contrast, I access Belonging to Interbeing through peace and awe. The parasympathetic branch of my nervous system yields belonging, when my individuality joins the web of life and death through my willing surrender.

There are many ways to cultivate a sense of willing surrender. I can cultivate surrender with my breath. With safe-enough space and time to breathe deeply, I turn my attention to the sparkle and hum of my body and soul. Noticing places of contraction and tension, I invite ease, and feel them open.

With breath enough, and time, awareness expands. I become integrated with a vast field, out beyond ideas. I'll meet you there.

We can explore the experience of surrender in lovemaking – beginning with an ongoing noticing of our own feeling states, as they are ever-changing. Centred in ourselves, we can open our eyes (and/or other body orifices), to take in another or others. Suddenly, awareness expands; energies interpenetrate. We surrender to receive each other. With an orgasmic feeling that goes on and on, we weave together into an us.

Journeying in a safe natural area with an entheogen, while holding the guiding intention of experiencing interbeing, feels like a transforming and deeply sacred practice. (The Greek adjective *entheos* translates to English as "full of the divine, inspired.") Psychedelic medicines including LSD, psilocybin, and other substances can be asked to encourage the dissolution of our egos, in sacred contexts. When focusing on Belonging to Interbeing, I like to create a ritual outdoors where I journey with a "psycholytic" dose (that is, enough medicine so that I can deepen into dialogue with the magic in the medicine, and also dialogue the natural world around me – as well as potentially holding council with other humans who join me in the ritual).

Lying down on the earth, I feel our unity. Dancing with grasses, I share our aliveness. In the forest, I rest against trees. They invite me to sing, and I listen to their stories. We are wild and wild is us.

MONARCH BUTTERFLY MEDITATION

On my medicine path of embodied love, the Monarch Butterfly inspires. Over and over, monarchs surrender to the web of life and death. They transform into new forms, and are born again. Eggs hatch into larvae that grow, and then pupate. Inside the pupal case, the larval body dies, melting into a molecular soup. Imaginal cells reach for one another, and form into the exoskeleton of a butterfly, then the molecules organize themselves into the new shape. The adult butterfly breaks open the pupal case, and learns to fly, then forms into great flocks with other butterflies. Together, they migrate across North America, for thousands of miles. But this is a multi-generational migration, with individual monarchs only making part of the journey.

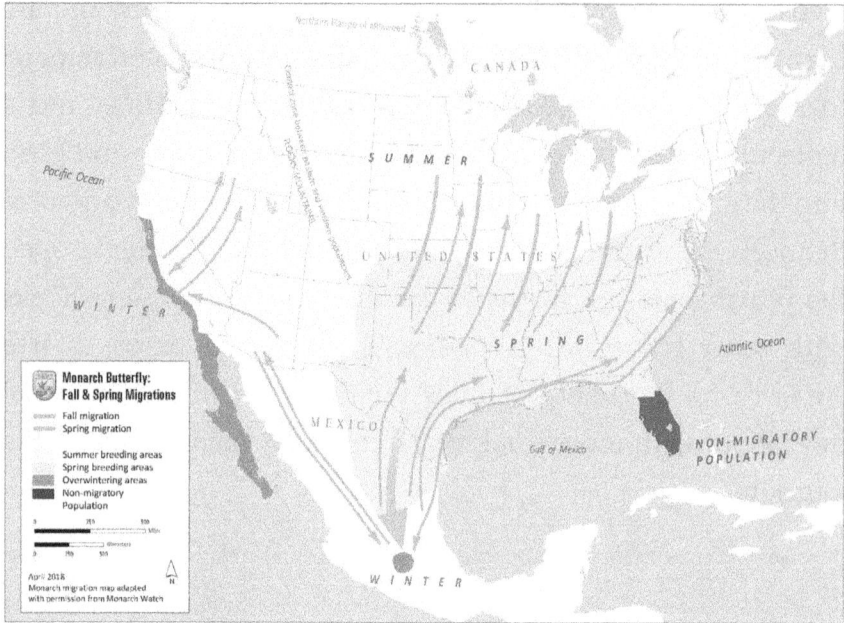

The multi-generational monarch butterfly migration of up to 3,000 miles goes from southern Canada to Central Mexico. Image by USFWS, CC

DEATH PREPARATION RITUAL

This ritual can be done as a large-scale rite of passage, with the support of guides, medicine and community. It can also be done as an everyday evening orientation to the nighttime world of sleep and dreams.

Create a ritual that invites your own experience of metamorphosis. Spend some time preparing for the ritual by consciously ending your orientation to acquiring more. This reorientation can be both physical and metaphorical. You might stop eating for awhile, stop purchasing and preparing things, and stop orienting to the future. Let yourself feel lost for a little while, as you prepare to surrender all you know.

In your lostness, you might start to notice the emergence of barely-discernable possibility: could there be a new version of you, that you don't yet know how to embody? You might start to feel as if this new version of you could, somehow, someday, be welcomed. The time has come to pupate. Create a pupa for yourself – perhaps in a hammock in a forest. You might want to bury yourself in dead leaves, or climb into bed, wrapped up in a blanket.

Inside your pupal case, let yourself dissolve. Let all the ways you know how to be and belong dissolve into nothing but a soup of molecules. Imagine that all the matter of you has no more shape, longing or purpose. What, in this soup of molecules, remains? Let your imaginal cells offer your molecules a new dream of you. Let these hitherto ignorable cells slowly take on the shape of a whole new you.

Imagine coming into this new way of being, and then, finding others like you, and flying and fucking together. Imagine your body delighted, and then, getting ragged and tired. Feel yourself coming to an end. What do you want to continue, in the generation that comes after you? How can you die into an ongoing becoming?

MORE QUEERING OF BINARIES

Part of belonging to interbeing, for me, is commitment to a continual querying and queering of binaries that separate me from the web of life and death that is the biosphere.

Capitalist, colonial culture generates a binary between human and nonhuman, along with an ever-contested boundary between them. Queer people have been made to dwell outside the margins of "humanity," alongside other two-leggeds deemed not-human, and all our biological elders, including birds, plants, fungus, microbes and frogs. Those of us deemed not-fully-human can get preoccupied with seeking enfranchisement. What if we instead make space to imagine ourselves outside the human-nonhuman binary? Who and how might we be, without this binary and its harmful impacts?

There is another either-or binary between life and death. The life-death binary robs us of ancestors. It separates us from the non-biotic world we are enmeshed in.

Zero or One
Binary Systems
Classical Computing

0 ◯

1 ●

0

Zero and One
plus all parts in and between
Nonbinary Systems
Quantum Computing

1

When a binary model of either-or is replaced by the
quantum truth of both-and, we multiply power

As a part of deepening my belonging to interbeing, I connect with queer ancestors, human and non-human, biotic and non-biotic. Outside our impoverished ideas of human lineage, in contradiction to the capitalist, colonial paradigm that describes every living thing as striving to protect, aggrandize and reproduce itself, there is a queer lineage of the miraculous. It is a lineage of love.

In my life, I find love enough to go on becoming me through courageous queer writers, friends and activists, as well as through specific trees, one-of-a kind animal companions, particular mountains and forests, the eccentric earth, and the singular universe itself. Support for queerness is passed down through all the ancestors who make a lineage that values uniqueness, while enjoying non-reproductive sexualities.

Can contemplating the idea of "queer ancestors," or attending or creating a "Queer Ancestors Ritual,"[11] resource you in belonging to interbeing? With a ritual that honours the magic of queerness, and our queer ancestors' courage and resilience, we can notice how we are influenced, inspired, wounded and resourced.

I like to focus on specific plants, each year at this time, and explore ways plants can be teachers and lovers. I spend time with them, draw and eat them, as I listen to their stories. Specific animals feel like power animals, with qualities of magic and medicine that resonate with my soul. Mapping a

---

11 Daka Ziji and Jackson Wai Chung Tse brought a Queer Ancestry Ritual to my studio in 2022. These rituals are a group contemplation and enactment of a queer cosmology, exploring: "Why does queerness exist?" "What is queerness?" going through the lineage of queers of today, queers in tolerant cultures, queers of intolerant cultures, queer animals and plants, the queer earth and the queer breath of the universe.

matrix of interspecies relationships I feel embedded in, I grow an awareness that supports me in being who and how I want to be.

SKETCH AN INTERSPECIES RELATIONSHIP MAP

Who are your plant and animal allies and companions? Are there resources, teachings or groups that guide you in belonging to the more-than-human world?

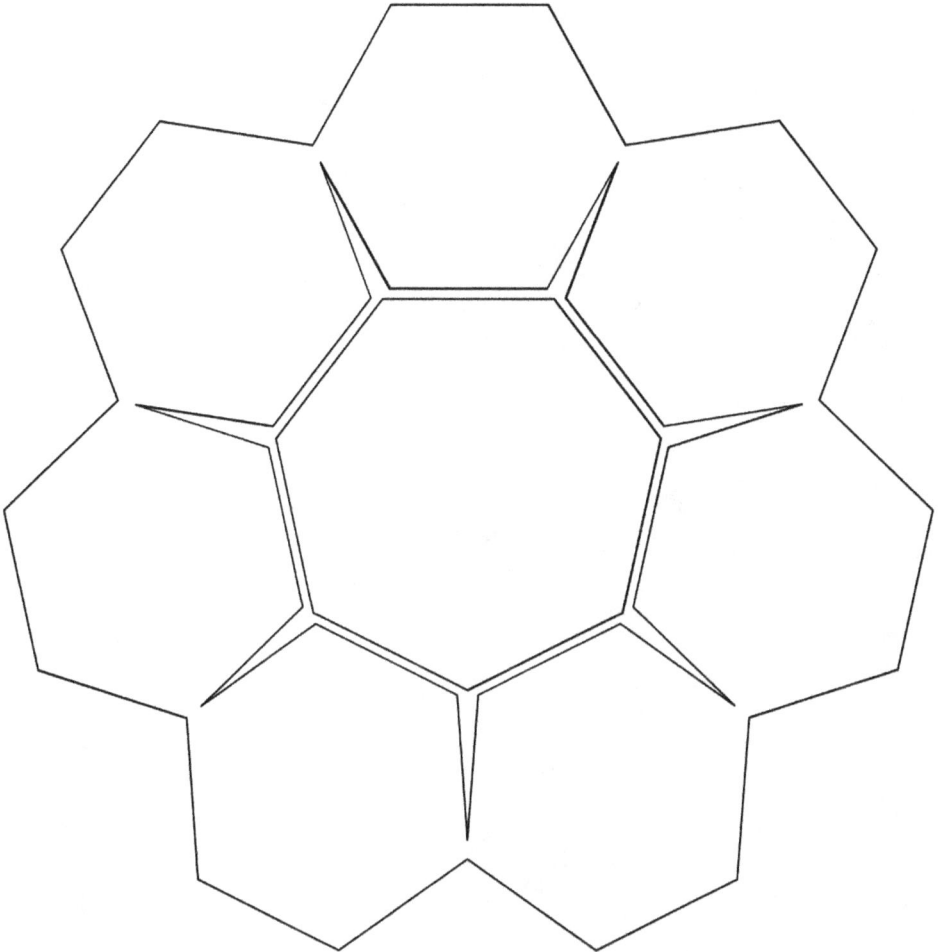

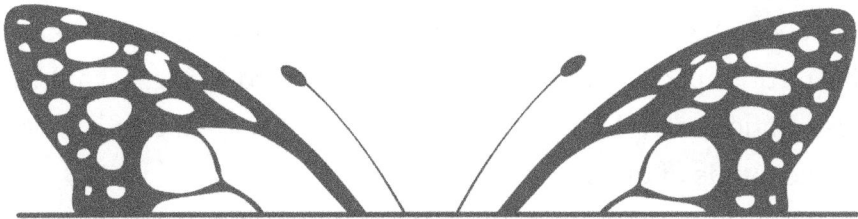

SEPTEMBER AND OCTOBER:
BELONGING TO REPAIR

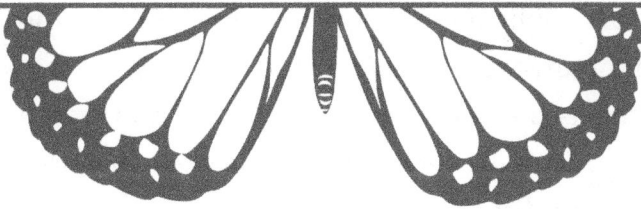

I belong to repair.

*I commit to repairing harm
I have done, whether intentionally
or unintentionally.
I commit to repair of harm done to me.*

Ethics for Outlaws

Ecosystems evidence a living ethics. In the wake of any experience of harm, they reach for repair. Repair is both an individual inclination and a system-level process we can witness all around us. In every broken branch and vacant lot, you'll find a reach for repair.

I want to be engaged in processes of ongoing repair, as I navigate my intimacies and communities. In September and October, shadows lengthen. It feels like a good time to look at harmful impacts I have, that I haven't wanted to see. I want to also notice harm I have experienced – by my own hands, and at the hands of others.

In the normative world of capitalism and colonialism, we are scared of our own shadows – for good reason. We deny and hide our shadows, because our belonging is always partial and provisional. Community is comprised by outlawing all who offend. Public humiliation, mob violence, the torture and exclusion of anyone who is deemed to transgress some social norm… this is the relentless experience of family, village and community through centuries of European history. Tarring and feathering, being ridden out of town on a rail, pillories, shame parades, public burning and drowning – all key to the biopolitic that Europeans brought to their colonies. In this regime, "communities" are no more than aggregations of individuals, where each one of us metabolizes reasonable terrors of running afoul of social norms.

Being declared an outlaw was the harshest possible penalty that could be meted out by the societies of premodern Europe. An outlaw does not deserve the protection of law and can be killed with impunity. We become outlaws one at a time – and it is a lonely and terrifying experience.

We live in fear of betrayal and abandonment, dread that we are unlovable, certain knowledge that my bad or your bad endangers me, terror that I am not good enough. We all engage in continual self-management so that unwelcome parts of us stay hidden. We are so afraid of being found out, and being punished, stigmatized, outlawed. We feel health and success in the oh-so-pleasant feeling of conforming enough to privileged social norms that we can relax awhile, and enjoy a deeper breath. Multiple, intersecting oppressions make sure no one is unafraid. Everyone sees how precarious and conditional all belonging is, and so we live in threat management, guided by fear.

I am a sex worker, a queer person and an explorer of illegal medicines. I am autistic. I am old. These are just some of the reasons I've been banished from the world of normative belonging, and considered an outlaw. I also can see – from my space of white privilege – how patterns of othering and outlawing are woven with property law, criminal law, policing and the legal system, so that white people are protected while Black and Indigenous people, and other people of colour, live in mortal danger. Hierarchies of precarity and privilege are generated by the "protection racket" of the so-called justice system. We need commitment to co-creating radical alternatives, and a patient practice in growing our personal and community capacities to understand justice, safety and repair in new ways.

When the criminal justice system will certainly harm us, and conventional morality precludes us, what happens when we get into an ethical quagmire? We likely have no way to reach out for help and guidance, and no community oversight for processes of reconciliation and repair.

I have witnessed counternormative communities made dangerous by intimate partner violence, financial abuse, and sexual abuse, and there have been no community processes for guiding accountability and repair. I've seen community belonging withdrawn over seeming trivialities: personality differences; gossip; bad breakups; mismanaged arguments, and there's been no process for containing the damage. People exercise unconscious entitlements and old traumas get triggered. There are deeply harmful impacts. But do we need to mimic dominant culture patterns of creating community by denying belonging to those who are bad and wrong? Or can we co-create communities that structurally and passionately want and welcome learning? How can we hold people in a cauldron that supports them in being with their vulnerabilities, while we grow capacities for centred accountability for harm done, and for repair?

On the path I walk, and in the resources I offer, I am guided by the Black-led movement for Transformative Justice. This social movement is rooted in communities of colour, queer lives, sex worker activism and disability justice. What is justice for people who are targeted and punished by the existing system of law, policing and imprisonment? Transformative Justice is a movement that creates space, and specific practices, for imagining and co-creating new social worlds. We learn to address harm without turning to the violent systems that increase it.

Can we co-create a social environment where we call one another in to accountability for harmful impacts, without calling for separation and banishment? Can we learn to welcome mistakes as opportunities for learning? Can we manifest an ongoing discernment of what is and is not rectifiable? Can we embody an ethic of zero waste, as we track the emergence and divergence of real differences? Can we begin to dismantle hierarchies of precarity and privilege, and address historic injustice?

BEYOND SHAME AND BLAME

Neuroscience tells us that when we feel angry, scared, hurt or overwhelmed, our brains generate stories of shame and blame. Such stories function as signals there is unsafety; there is work to be done. But they are stories of separation. If we want to create communities where we can be courageous, celebrate difference, make mistakes, learn and grow, and create new worlds together, then getting stuck in shame and blame is mean and demeaning.

As a teacher and practitioner of sacred intimacy, I have seen, again and again, how shame has a corrosive impact on our living, learning and loving. Choices, identities and ways of being that bring people into contradiction with community norms can leave them feeling full of shame and unlovable. Experiences of powerlessness, in the overwhelm of lonely traumas, often leave people feeling mired in shame. In these instances, shame is an attachment wound that can be healed by love. We need healing holding environments, and caring community. There is a different kind of shame that people feel when their actions take them out of alignment with their *own* truth and dignity, and how they want to show up in intimate relationships and in community. This kind of shame is a call to personal integrity. Its discomforts can serve a truing mechanism that supports us in healing personal failures, and growing brave enough to make amends.

As contributors to courageous communities where shame is healed, we see again and again how corrosive blame wants to divide us. People might try to get rid of a "bad apple" to regain community equilibrium – while failing to generate relational wellness and undo systemic oppressions. The same power dynamics keep arising, and the same dramas get played out, again and again. Other folks create profound harm by bringing intimate relationship misattunements into the community realm, wreaking havoc by trying to mobilize others' resentments. Yet understanding "who is to blame" is sometimes relevant to personal and community wellness, as we clear a path for centered accountability, and living amends.

These issues are always complex, but I think we can all recognize "Plumb Lines" of personal and community wellness. We can actually *feel* where we are being pulled out of right relationship with ourselves and others by shame and blame. The courageous individualities we have fostered and the caring communities we live and love in are far too precious to poison. Let's go beyond shame and blame as ways to manage conflict.

BEYOND SHAME

DIGNITY

Trauma or
Mistakes
Causing
Injury

Abandoning
the Self
or Shared
Values

Love as
Community
Work

Plumb Line of Personal Wellness

Love as
Individual
Work

Reassurance

Learning

Expanded
Belonging

Amends

Personal
Integrity

Gratitude

HUMILITY

BEYOND BLAME

THE MOLECULAR LANGUAGE OF ECOSYSTEMS

Ecosystems around the world have molecular messengers, so that each independently-existing being can find right relationship between its own needs and longings, and those of community. As I focus on belonging to repair, I feel resourced by my conscious embodiment of the neuroendocrine system that is common to all life.[12] This molecular system is the one we consciously augment, and bring into balance, as we engage in ecstatic practices, and work with psychedelic medicines.

Every unique being within an ecosystem needs to accept constraints on its individual life, and feel respect and self-respect inside those limits. There are molecules called indolemines that carry this message: auxin, serotonin, melatonin, DMT.

At the same time, each being also needs to be empowered by something quite opposite to acceptance. Each one needs courage and capacity, so it can live into its longings and bear its agony. Each one needs daring and desire, to give it strength to rise, and engage in opportunities for requisite divergence, and true partnership. Other molecules called catecholemines – including dopamine and adrenaline – partner with steroid hormones like cortisol and sex steroids to empower courageous and purposeful living.

Ecosystems want and need each one in a community to be empowered to accept grief and agony, and still feel longing and joy, so we can each and all stay committed to living and dying in love together. Each one needs to be able to expand into the fierce eudaimonic pleasures of living on purpose, and simultaneously find and feel the contentments of daily care and kindness. Peptide hormones and neuropeptides foster these capacities within individuals, and between all those who touch

12 In describing the neurochemistry of ecosystems, I am simplifying a complexity that is intricate and intimate. There are hundreds of signalling molecules moving through different domains, phyla, families, genera, and species. Every signalling molecule can have multiple effects, depending on context. By simplifying, and focusing on comprehensible contradictions that particular molecules empower us to embody, I hope to land in some version of emergent truth. This information is also included and discussed in *Love and Death*.

each other within an ecosystem. In animals, magnocellular oxytocin empowers mad love – risk-taking, passion, impossible somatic openings, like the opening of the cervix before a baby is birthed. It stretches us into the hitherto unthinkable and impossible. Parvocellular oxytocin floods a body with everyday goodwill and welcome, in response to the feeling of belonging, and safe and wanted touch. It lets us savour the sweetness of love, and act lovingly, with grounded presence. Endorphins manage the extremes of agony and ecstasy; they catapult us out beyond ourselves, into transcendent interbeing.

If catecholamines and steroids get out of balance with indolemines and peptides, we might need the help of culture, community and molecular guides. I certainly need ongoing guidance from molecular medicines, and sacred ceremony. I need to keep on discerning where I have done harm, and listening to those who are courageous enough to want a better version of me, so we can keep on co-creating home together.

Neuroendocrine System of Ecosystems

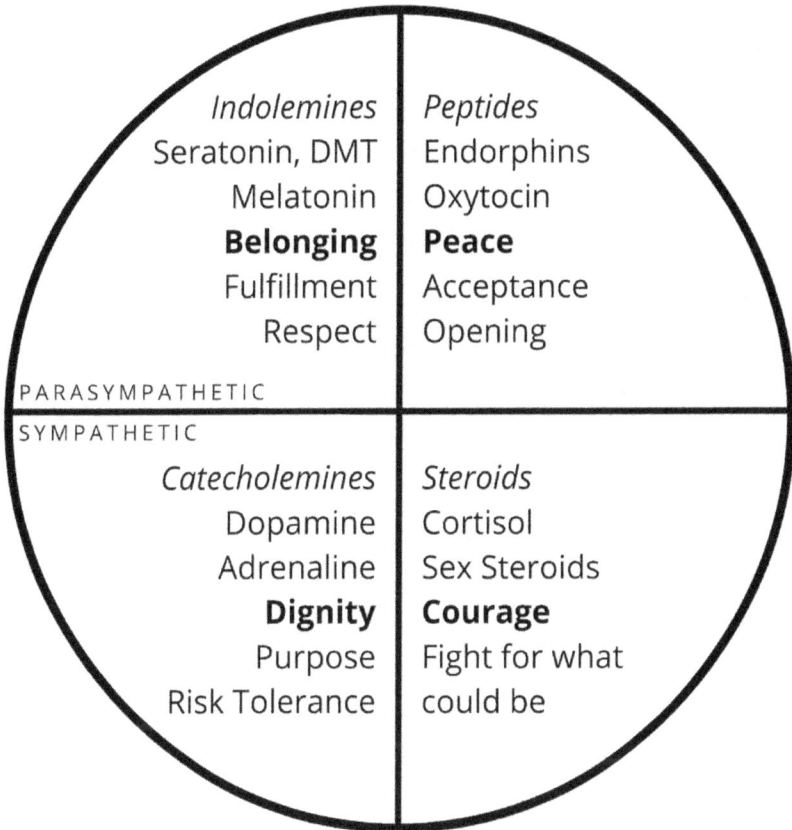

Indolemines	*Peptides*
Seratonin, DMT	Endorphins
Melatonin	Oxytocin
Belonging	**Peace**
Fulfillment	Acceptance
Respect	Opening

PARASYMPATHETIC

SYMPATHETIC

Catecholemines	*Steroids*
Dopamine	Cortisol
Adrenaline	Sex Steroids
Dignity	**Courage**
Purpose	Fight for what
Risk Tolerance	could be

Ecosystems developed a neuroendocrine system we share with all life, and the life-after-death of humic compounds in soil. Each being, and the conspiracy of beings that co-creates the biosphere, can feel and follow its longing for even more ecstasy. It can follow its contradictory longing for peace and equilibrium. Our longings – and the contradictions between them – are trustworthy, when we are anchored in a place and a process that regularly and wonderfully feels like home. Home is the body of each one of us, feeling our resilience and integrity, held in the ephemeral web of belonging that is true intimacy. Home is interbeing. Home is an emergence of a shared commitment to repair, in our counternormative communities of imperfect practice.

Dignity, courage, peace and belonging are not empty words. These are embodied states that can be felt and experienced, within and between us. Dignity and courage pull us up into our full height. Peace and belonging stretch us wide. We feel the contradictory pulls: between opposite sides of our nervous system, between opposite tendencies in our attachment patterns, between what's right for me and what works for us. We offer each other trustworthy, gentle, supported traction, and passionate and compassionate love, so we can stretch into the contradictions just a little more.

Learning, community and culture – along with ecstatic practices and sacred medicines – can guide and resource us. Without them, we might forgo the stretch. We might truncate our courage to find belonging, or forgo belonging to preserve our dignity. We might make intimacies small enough so we can meet at the lowest common denominator in our attachment patterns. We could be tempted to hide the agonies in our economy. In social and ecological relationships, we might look to find ease and excitement through privileges assumed at others' expense.

With community, culture, sacred medicines and regular ecstasies to resource our molecular learning, we can want and welcome the feeling of opposing forces stretching us. We know to devote time to frisky friction, and let the tensions build, until the amplified energy fractures every space of ease within and between us. Our dignity can be engorged, and our courage conjured. We can want, allow and encourage bodies, intimacies, and ecosystems to feel conflicting pushes and pulls, until we reach a climax state of maximum differentiation, and follow small and large orgasmic cascades into unity. We can pay attention to the pleasure of each and every climax, letting the ecstasy of it rock and shape us. In the afterglow, we can savour deep peace, and feel true belonging. This is home.

ON DESERVINGNESS

I don't deserve to live… I don't deserve love…

Rather than rushing to reassure me, why not join me? Let's jettison the notion of deservingness, and dance in our undeservingness. Perhaps I can even find a mischievous relish in my unworthiness…. if you can enjoy it too. Perhaps I will better experience the improbable miracle of living and being loved, when I acknowledge the random luck of it. How astonishing, that I am alive! What undeserved grace I find – that this weird, wild one I am – with all my flaws and splendours – is loved by the one who is uniquely you!

Deservingness implies a calculus of relative worth. Etymologically, it means "to serve completely" – the word was coined to honour worthy servants of the wealthy. We get feelings of deserving through our serving. We can look to colonialism and capitalism, then, to understand how the feeling of "deservingness" became so foundational to our sense of wellness – taking root in our regard for self and other, and growing power enough to shape our dreams.

When Indigenous North American explorers and intellectuals first traveled to Europe, they were appalled by the savagery they found there. Never could they have imagined people so unkind. They described the huge economic inequalities as deeply shocking. In sharp contrast to Indigenous societies, European social organization distributed wealth through grotesque differentiations of rich from poor.

Capitalist, colonial culture, language, education and religion all work to root rank deep inside us, with binary notions of deserving and undeserving, human and non-human, male and female, white and non-white, and on and on.... What if deservingness doesn't parse into an either-or binary, any more than gender, race or sexuality? What if deservingness can it be better understood as one choice among many, in a fluid and everchanging spectrum of choices that give resilience to social and spiritual life? We can be deserving, through epic serving, and we can also accept, take and allow, without expectation or entitlement (as Betty Martin so beautifully guides).

I want to belong to repair of harm I have done – intentionally and unintentionally – without being overwhelmed by my unworthiness. There is no way to ever feel deserving, as a white person addressing racial harms. In any intersection where I have privilege, I need to stop believing I somehow deserve it – that I am worth it. So too, I need to stop believing that being undeserving makes me unlovable, or requires perpetual punishment. Over-attachment to the paradigm of deservingness feeds fragility, separation and inaction. I want to belong to repair – not to earn my worthiness, but because repair thrills my soul. Repair is the language of ecosystems and ancestors. It is the song of the biosphere, living through me.

GENERATIVE CONFLICT

How do we deal with conflict, while we go on making a world where differences between us can be welcomed and delighted in? Can conflict be a way to generate more love, and complex community? Can we learn to hold conflict as an integral part of social transformation and belonging in communities that value difference?

When we feel danger, we are not neurologically resourced for creative engagement. How can we engage in conflict, then, in ways that honour the resourced responsibility and tender care that are key to us? I created the "Generative Conflict Map" with friends and colleagues, to serve as a preliminary map to orient us, when conflict startles, frightens and threatens us. A more complex colour version of this map, along with writings about each step, are offered as free resources on my website. May these resources assist us in opening space and time for living an ethics based on joy and justice.

This Generative Conflict Map is a guide to traversing an imaginary space where conflict happens between equals. There is no such space, and so the work of being responsible to power dynamics becomes integral to any conflict process. We can honour the authentic vulnerabilities of all involved with attention to privilege and precarity. How are we learning to use any privilege we hold in the service of what we care about? We are biophysically incapacitated in different ways by precarity. Conscious navigation of inequalities is essential.

Generative Conflict Map

Rest and Integrate
Harvest Learning
(7)

Find Holding
Anchor Belonging
(1)

Explore Emergence
Supported
Soul Inquiry
(2)

Co-Create Ritual
Community Process
(6)

Spin Story
History and Context
(3)

Queer Conflict
Go beyond binaries
(5)

Pick your battles
Consider costs and scale
(4)

A colour poster-sized PDF of this map, and detailed reflections on each step, are available through the "Transformative Justice" page of EcstaticBelonging.com. This map was created with Tricia Bowler and Kai Cheng Thom, in the creative cauldron of the Institute for the Study of Somatic Sex Education.

APOLOGY RITUAL

The "Apology Ritual" is offered here as an experimental process for addressing harm through ritual. This ritual originated with Tricia Bowler. In the last few years, she and I have worked together to explore its relevance, and shape it into the form shared here. Using the Apology Ritual has been fruitful for us, in counternormative community spaces in which all people involved are actively committed to accountability, embodied love and social permaculture. Having occasional large-scale ritual experiences also helps us to stay in an everyday practice of belonging to repair. We seek to be 100% accountable for our own part, in the many situations where we have unintended harmful impacts, and want to reach for repair. Within the ritual itself, we forgo defending ourselves by claiming equal injury, figuring out who is to blame, finding folks who agree someone else is wrong, and ruminating on all our reasons.

With the Apology Ritual, we aim to co-create ritual space in which:

- our souls can meet each other, and learn and teach each other
- the impact of harmful behaviours can be fully felt and shared
- the impact of systemic oppressions can be shared and better understood
- the creative power that gets manifested at the site of injuries can be honoured and shared
- people can understand harm they have done from a place of centred accountability

- people can commit to living differently, and feel resourced for living amends
- role play can be used to explore injury and accountability in a contained, supportive context

There are three main participants in the process, who take on three different roles. An audience can be invited to witness. This can be a personal apology, or a transpersonal exploration. Personal and transpersonal often mix together in the ritual; injury and accountability have dimensions that extend back in time before our birth, and around the world to others like us. Whenever a man is apologizing to a woman, a person with white privilege is apologizing to a racialized person, or a heterosexually-privileged person is apologizing to a queer person (to offer just three examples) we want to be sure to anchor in history and context, and evoke transpersonal dimensions in our ritual.

1. **Celebrant:** Creates ritual container, and guides the process.

2. **Injured One:** Reflects on woundedness with courage, to acknowledge harm done to them, and the ongoing impact. Reaches for understanding of the creative power they manifest from these injuries. Receives reassurance of their innocence, with soul honouring, and the Apologizer's commitment to living amends.

3. **Apologizer:** Stands centred in a commitment to expressing 100% accountability, without any defensiveness. Reaches for soul-deep curiosity, and longing to hear of the harmful impacts of what they have done and failed to do. Apologizes from a resourced place, with capacity for authentic social engagement.

Understands and honours the other's innocence. Learns of the other's medicine. Commits to a path of living amends.

The ritual begins with the Apologizer stating their commitment to stand in 100% accountability. In this context, the Injured One is asked to share as much as they want to share, of the impacts on them of this injury: on their health, relationships, career, family. Each impact is met with accountability. "I apologize for that. It was my fault alone. You are completely innocent."

After the injury has been fully expressed, the Celebrant asks: "Would you be willing to share with us what medicines have you created from your experience?" The Injured One then has a chance to speak about new wisdoms and practices that emerged from the injury. (This is a delicate inquiry, as we do not want to ever excuse harm, or imagine that injury builds character. And yet, if our souls survive the violences, we can generate new superpowers in the cauldron of trauma.)

Having heard about the injury, and medicines created from them, the Apologizer asks "What living amends do you want from me?" They make a commitment to living amends.

At the end of the ritual, participants de-role. Outside the roles assumed for the ritual, they reflect what they are harvesting, and how they feel transformed.

Post-Apology Opportunities and Cautions

The Injured One may feel deeply vulnerable after allowing and sharing the extent of injury they felt. They may need extra support.

The Apologizer may find themselves slipping into overwhelming shame or defensiveness. They may need extra support.

All participants in the ritual need to track the ongoing unfolding of right relationship with each other, and with the ritual experience. Are the roles assumed – and the vulnerable information shared – safely contained within the ritual? If the Apology Ritual is not held as a contained process, there is danger that roles and information can be weaponized.

The commitment to a caring community is what creates context, opportunity and efficacy for the ritual. All members of the community can be invited to notice, share and ask participants about what is transformed by the ritual. "How are we changed by this? How are we understanding harmful impacts, and respecting diverse wisdoms? How are we living amends?"

Empathogens to Resource Apologies

MDMA and 3-MMC are molecular medicines that help me hydrate emotionally. I can deepen my "Belonging to Repair," with their help. I have molecular support enough to put down my defensiveness, and slow down my habitual ways of relating in conflict. Threat management behaviours of fight, flight, freeze and appease feel much less necessary. I get grounded in my longing for – and commitment to – more and better love; I can reach past strategic fixes and problem-solving. At some point during the months when I am focusing on "Belonging to Repair," I like to reach for the help of one of these molecular guides, and create a ritual inquiry.

I hope that we can find safe-enough, brave-enough ways to seek guidance from these medicines, as we deepen into repairing ancestral trauma, and addressing the ongoing harms of oppressive systems.

NOVEMBER AND DECEMBER: BELONGING TO NONBEING

I belong to nonbeing.

*I integrate spaciousness, as I weave
my self into the web of life and death.*

CLIMATE CHAOS AND MASS EXTINCTION

As the year comes to a close, in November and December, I focus on Belonging to Nonbeing. I want to deepen into this facet of belonging, in part because I am old. I want to belong to my own death. I also want to belong to a biosphere that is experiencing climate chaos and mass extinction. Around the world, there is so much suffering and death.

Facing the truth of this time on planet earth is an enormous task. How can we make space enough inside us, to really notice? How can we be with our immense grief, as we experience the unbearable losses that are everywhere unfolding? How can we metabolize our overwhelming fear? With each new demagogue elected, failed climate initiative, and day of relentless rain or smoke-filled sky, we lurch towards the tipping point. Despite all our passion, longing, and the beauty and intrigue of our stories, we hover in the instability of an evermore imminent end. If the immensity of suffering, grief and fear is fully felt, how can we stay conscious? If we let ourselves notice all that is betrayed, and forever lost, of the biosphere's exuberant, intricate magic, how can we still choose love?

Capitalism and colonialism teach us to deny death, armour ourselves against nonbeing, and dissociate in the presence of suffering. On the medicine path of embodied love, we can learn to stay present to suffering, belong to death, and integrate nonbeing into our very being. We can prepare to die in ways that embody love, and make space to imagine the ongoing emergence of life-giving love, even in life-after-death. At the very least, this path can resource us with peace and joy, as we navigate so many agonizing ends.

PRESENCE WITH SUFFERING

In the shock of trauma, there is a moment when hyperactivated nervous systems reach a zenith of panic. Suddenly, we experience a dorsal-vagal drop. We abandon our selves. It is as if there is no more separate self to inhabit. We have no ground beneath our feet. There are no boundaries. There is no mind. We exit the storyline of linear time. We cannot act on our own behalf, flee, fight or cry for help. Heartbeat and breath slow down. Awareness of agony is dimmed. It is as if we die, before we die. Through dissociative self-abandonment, we escape being present with suffering.

It is so merciful that, in the immediacy of trauma, we die before we die. But what a loss, if we survive without integrating the impact of trauma – because then we live half-dead, numbed and atomized. Everyone has their own story. For me, there was a violent sexual assault by a stranger, when I was nine months old, along with a sustained experience of family violence. Dissociative self-abandonment mercifully truncated my suffering. But without context, companionship and culture to hold me so I could mend, dissociation became a lifelong neuroendocrine habit. Like so many others, in a world where trauma and neglect are ordinary and untended, my biorhythms were muted. My body and soul contracted and collapsed; my neuroendocrine system cycled within constraints that kept me from the extremes of feeling fully. Agonies were muted, along with ecstasies. I could not be present with suffering.

I was in my sixties before I found context and support enough to come all the way home to my body again. In the arms of lover earth, with the help of psychedelic medicine, somatic sexual wellness, a well-guided temple of courageous companions, and a life full of loving friends, I finally laid still and remembered my infant body being helpless, violated and overwhelmed. I could feel my own embodied kinship with the suffering of lover earth, and all the many beings suffering upon it. I could be present with suffering, because I know I am not alone. We each have a singular story of suffering, and we belong to a biosphere where there is so much suffering. By knowing we are not alone in it, we can each learn to hold our own in it. Together, we can be present with suffering; we can make it our own.

There is an actual neuroendocrine experience of embodied unity, and we can weave it. Loving relationships, counternormative understandings, somatic practices and psychedelic medicines all help unite us in the experience of embodied love. In love, over time, we can ease out of our atomizing contractions and isolating collapses. We can reach back in time, to hold the suffering of human and more-than-human ancestors. We can reach forward in time, to hold the suffering to come. Together, we can discern the nested pink noise rhythms in which extremes of agony and ecstasy can be held.

PINK NOISE SYSTEMS

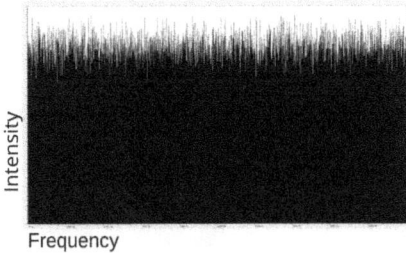

White Noise
All sounds exist equally. The most intense sounds are muted, and subtle sounds are overwhelmed.

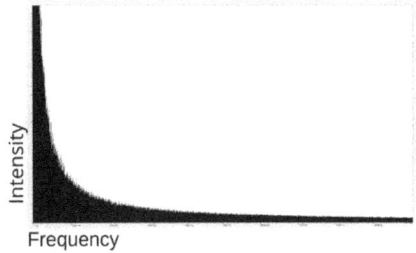

Pink Noise
All sounds exist at a frequency inversely proportional to their intensity.

Spectral analysis of white and pink noise. Adapted from Glenn Elert.

Extremes of agony and ecstasy seem like random noise, if we are isolated and alone. Together, in time, we can see how they belong, as part of resonant, integrated systems.

"White noise" means that a system's variety clusters around the average. All frequencies and amplitudes of energy exist equally, but subtle sounds are overwhelmed, and the most intense sounds muted.

"Pink noise" is the whole energy spectrum, oscillating together, with frequency inversely proportional to intensity. A long tail of low intensity oscillations is punctuated by extremely large, infrequent climaxes. Each octave interval (halving or doubling in frequency) comes to carry the same quantity of energy, over time.

Pink noise, also described as $1/f$ noise, is one of the most common characteristics of complex systems. The sun itself exhibits pink noise behaviour, as the magnitude of solar flares varies according to a 1/f power law. Energy coming from distant stars shows the same kind of variability. On earth, pink noise patterns have been discerned in the fluctuations of an extraordinarily diverse number of physical and biological systems: variations in tide and river heights; quasar light emissions; heart beat rhythms; neural activity; the statistics of DNA sequences.... Human music is like tides, not in terms of how the ocean sounds, but in the rhythms in which tide heights vary, over time. In every form of human music, and every comforting human voice in any language, there is a pink noise pattern.

Pink is a discernible rhythm that emerges in time, not all at once. To exist, it needs observers with patience and persistence. Great variety, unfolding at different timescales, seems random and unlearnable – if we don't slow down and give things time. With patient curiosity, and sustained attention, it turns out that this variety is what makes things pink. Earthquake frequency has the same pink patterns, at a different timescale, as plankton swarm behaviour, and population dynamics in predator-prey systems.

In every individual organism that lives into a full lifetime, there is a pink noise pattern. High intensity transformations of birth, early life initiations, the long-tail distribution of maturity and aging, and the calamity of death all unfold according to a rhythm that aligns us with ecosystem dynamics and the pulse of stars. Pink noise patterns emerge in every complex, climax ecosystem, in the distribution of species, and in relationships between individuals, species, and the system as a whole. The biosphere and our orgasms have the same pink rhythms.

If we want to be part of white noise systems, we should keep on asking "How can I be more normal?"

"How do I keep my most intense joys and agonies muted, and ignore all subtleties?"

If we want to sing Earthsong, and join in belonging to the rhythms of the universe, we will ask different questions:

"How can I lean into my eccentricities, and become more fully and uniquely me?"

"How can I cultivate capacity for staying present with experiences of great intensity, inside long arcs of subtle arousal, and gentle peace?"

Chaos Theory

In the fall of 2020, in the midst of a global pandemic, the air was filled with smoke from devastating wildfires. Communities around the world were riven with struggles for racial justice. The 33-acre forest next door to me was getting relentlessly clear-cut. The demands of my work, together with my awareness of the suffering being experienced by my students, felt overwhelming. I became increasingly ill, until one night I wound up at the hospital with heart pain, struggling for breath. I was diagnosed as having a chronic, terminal lung disease. For a few months, I faced my own imminent end.

My diagnosis was later reversed; two years later I was climbing trees, and feeling filled with aliveness. But during the months I thought I'd die quickly, I engaged in a focused inquiry into my own death. As part of my inquiry, I explored the psychedelic medicine 5meO-DMT with a trustworthy guide. 5meO-DMT is a powerful medicine that has been described as "the God molecule," and said to offer short experiences of dying.

Over a whole day spent in the guide's studio, I had a gentle introduction to the medicine, followed by a deeper dive in which I felt I was experiencing my own death. In a final round, I died into a transpersonal realm where there was no more me, and no more us. For 30 minutes of timeless time, there was only Chaos, nonbeing and nothingness.

Chaos is formlessness, before the beginning of time, outside the storyline of earth and universe, out beyond ideas. Chaos is dark and silent; it is peace. Chaos is seeded with mystery; there are strange attractors and glowing points of light. Chaos is right here, right now, inside and around us. It is a deep well of ongoing emergence, from which the never-before can suddenly come into being.

Chaos can be explained by quantum physics, but my language is erotic embodiment, and so I will explain it with the diagram below. We find our way to Chaos in post-orgasmic bliss. Chaos is the wild order of sleep and dreams, or falling in love, in which the unpredictable is ever-emerging. Before the beginning and after the end, Chaos is the liminal realm of timeless time, where tiny changes trigger profound consequences. When pattern and beauty emerge from Chaos, then there is Eros. There is something to love and lose. Longing for more, there is reason to learn. We resist disaggregation into Chaos; we follow a storyline.

We fear Chaos, and we armour ourselves against it, because Chaos brings an end to stories. In the silence of nonbeing and nothingness, we don't know how or whether we'll begin again. But if we better understand, practice and prepare for Chaos, we can learn to integrate it. We can take time in timeless time, to rest and to savour. We can delight in the mystery of Chaos. We can learn how spaciousness and emptiness host unknowable possibilities, and strange new elements.

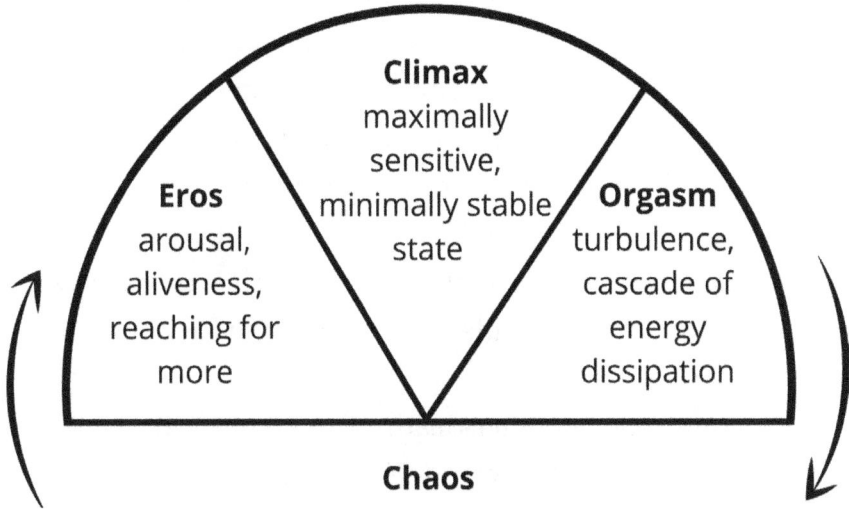

Climax
maximally
sensitive,
minimally stable
state

Eros
arousal,
aliveness,
reaching for
more

Orgasm
turbulence,
cascade of
energy
dissipation

Chaos

LIFE AFTER DEATH

I begin by honouring the many forms of life-after-death we already embody. Here are just five:

1. The stardust we are made of was formed in the death of a giant star. Simple stardust used the energy of a dying star to fuse into the complex elements of planet earth, including carbon, nitrogen and oxygen.

2. During embryonic development, our own unique genome takes on forms that die before we are born – including trophoblast, yolk sac and placenta. Like insects, we experience metamorphosis.

3. The molecules of plants and animals we eat become us.

4. Egg and sperm die into the creation of something wholly new, as they join to form the first cell of us. Each singular being that comes into being through a union of two gametes – that is, every plant, animal and fungus in the whole biosphere – embodies the life-after-death of two unique genomes, that are themselves different from our parents' genomes. (Processes of so-called reproduction are actually processes of deep differentiation, resourced by death.)

5. Disconnected cells within us are continually committing "cell suicide" through apoptosis. This process keeps making the molecules of life available for new cellular growth.

Reaching for life-after-death does not mean grasping for some doctrine that comes from outside us. It means remembering, listening, and opening into a knowing as old as the stardust we are made of. As we hover at the brink of extinction, we can consciously weave ourselves into the web of life and death, and life-after-death, around and within us.

My commitment to the path of embodied love empowers me, as I deepen into exploring nonbeing, chaos and conscious dying. Many experiences of orgasm resource me. I synchronize and resonate with pink noise biorhythms. I feel and find my way to many forms of ecstatic belonging. There is joy, peace, excitement and awe; there is terror and grief.

Conscious Dying Ritual

Whether death is ecstatic or traumatic, it yields an extinguishment of our singular selves. With death, our atoms and ions can return to their inarguable belonging.

At some point during the months I am focused on Belonging to Nonbeing, I want to create a ritual practice of conscious dying. The ritual can be simple and short. I have floated for an hour, in darkness, in water the same temperature as my skin. A conscious dying ritual can be social, and fun. I have participated in a group where we wrote our own obituaries, with each other's help. Much giggling was enjoyed! A ritual can engage the erotic, to explore and resource the expansion and contraction of the neuroendocrine system. I have co-created erotic ritual where I met Death as my lover. I have arranged a BDSM session, in which the receiving of bold sensation yielded my deep, willing surrender.

I hope we can inspire each other with the wild, weird rituals we create, as we practice dying.

Beyond the "Window of Tolerance"

Between hope and despair, there's a "Window of Tolerance" where danger is managed. You feel safety in the world around you, and inside your skin.[13] Therapists all get trained to support clients in accessing and expanding a personal Window of Tolerance, so they can better navigate the everyday world. The theory goes like this.

When we have unmetabolized trauma, our bodies are awash with cortisol and adrenaline. We feel chronically unsafe. We might always feel hostile and hypervigilant (stuck in fight and flee responses), or forever depressed, exhausted, overwhelmed (stuck in freeze and appease responses). We might bounce around in a pinball machine of reactive

13 First described by Dan Siegel

energies – one day rageful, collapsing the next. With enough understanding, support, and embodied practice, we can shift our inner neuroendocrine environment. We can learn to live with more ease and efficacy, as we expand our neural Window of Tolerance. If we get the tools and we practice, our neuroendocrine system will calm down. We'll get better at tolerating the world, and feeling tolerated within it.

The Window of Tolerance is a helpful framework, and it sort-of works – but there is one enormous obstacle. The unloving, punitive, dangerous world of normative belonging grows evermore intolerable. We actually *are* chronically and increasingly unsafe, as the ongoing violences of capitalism and colonialism rage on, throughout the biosphere. Danger is here and now; there is no safe place. And so my medicine path is not about tolerance. It's about transformation.

How can we dream of profound social change, and reach for it, in ways that don't create more danger? How can we stop being dangerous to one another? We need to grow capacity to stay centered and effective, in expanded states of high arousal, so we can find courage enough to change the things we can. We need to grow capacity for grief's relentless agonies, and staying present with suffering, to accept what we cannot change.

With love and longing enough, I know we can grow these more spacious parts of our neuroendocrine system – both personally and collectively. Moreover, growing capacity for transformation does not mean bending our backs to yet another list of lonely chores. It's about feeling our way to real, resonant belonging. Reorienting to the neuroendocrine feedback loop that grows an evermore miraculous world, we'll find empowerment in our souls and relationships. We'll feel kinship and twinship, with all the other miracles unfolding throughout the biosphere. We'll feel at one with the love we already know and embody, in our stardust, cells, souls and skin.

By weaving erotic, ecstatic practices into our activism, we can grow familiar with the outer edges of our neuroendocrine system. We can feel resourced by familiarity with extraordinary ecstatic states, where we exceed all sense of being a separate self, and linger in the void that we all come from.

There are many ecstatic paths to dropping awareness of our separate selves, and coming home to nonbeing and nothingness. Despair can also take us there. Despair takes us down into the dorsal-vagal drop of knowing we can't change this. There is no escape. We abandon hope, and drop into the hell of the trauma that is irrevocably unfolding.

Going down into despair is tortuous and agonizing. But once we get all the way there, we find a place of peace. Acceptance is relief; it stems the grief. Numbness descends, to end the agony. If we savour the calmness of Chaos, it creates an energy gradient. Some unpredictable spark, sometime, is going to fly in.

We can practice despairing every night, with every nap, as we settle into letting go of doing one more thing. Just for now, there is nothing more that can be done, to save the world.... so let's take time to surrender all our stories, and dissolve into the dark. That's how we get calm enough to invite the world of dreams.

By inhabiting the full spectrum of our neuroendocrine system, we can come home to nonbeing and nothingness. We can come home through expansion, and the portal of ecstasy.

We can go through contraction, into deep despair, and arrive at that same home.

Nonbeing is not the enemy of being. It is the matrix of all being: mother, lover, friend. Between hope and despair, let's choose both.

WALKING EACH OTHER HOME

The spirit of suicidality has been a companion for me, all my life. Now it seems to haunt the whole world, in such harmful, unconscious ways. I want to find ways to acknowledge that spirit, and work with it more consciously and carefully.

In my early life, I struggled to escape the spirit of suicidality, and resist its guidance. I wanted to die, but I wanted to live! How could my opposite longings ever be reconciled? Growing old, I've learned to belong to my longing to extinguish my singularity, and come to an end. I've learned how my longing can be satisfied through ecstasies. I've also learned to dance with my despair. Imagining my own end serves as a truing mechanism; it helps me feel and accept my limits, and choose the next steps that are right for me.

I want to honour those I love, human and non-human, who have already chosen to end their lives. They demonstrate how death can be a positive choice, to go home to the matrix of nonbeing we all come from. If only each suicidal person could choose death while feeling cherished, companioned and deeply loved. If only they could grow familiar with the portal of ecstasy, as well as despair, so they knew they had choice in which path to follow, to find their way home. If only they could die knowing that the life they lived, and the death they chose, are a deep well of ongoing emergence, in a world where we are all walking each other home.

How differently could we approach the tipping point of the biosphere's unravelling, if we inhabited the full spectrum of our personal and interpersonal neuroendocrine system, and befriended both despair and ecstasy? As long as we stay scared of despair, we'll have to metabolize so much turmoil, anxiety, fear and pain. Will we get stuck, then, in the neuroendocrine feedback loop of creating an evermore dangerous world? Do we keep on grasping at straws, with ever-increasing panic? What if we just let go? I wonder where a collective experience of despair can land us.

Letting go of all that could have been, should have been. Releasing all our longings. Not now. Maybe never. Too little. Too late. No hope here. Let's breathe into hopelessness together. No more fighting, just the spaciousness and peacefulness of utter despair. Let's take another few moments: just this. Nothing to do or feel. Nowhere to go. Just the blessed emptiness of hopelessness, we hold between us, knowing.....

> The dark is enough,
> and the end.
> So let's love it, and linger.
> Silent, still, deeply satisfied until....
> a spark of light
> is enough
> to begin.

THE END IS THE BEGINNING

The oroborus – a snake eating its tail – is an image that appears in many cultures around the world, as a symbol of the unity of being and nonbeing. It's thought to have a specific origin in time. 7000 years ago, there were many globally independent observations of intense aurora that moved down towards the equator, and circled the earth like a snake eating its tail, during a time when the electromagnetic field of the planet quieted, and then suddenly, reversed. Perhaps in a time of mass despair

– or mass ecstatic practice – the planet's electromagnetic field can join us, and guide us, into a reversal of everything that looks unchanging and inevitable....

Can our reach for rapture and surrender to despair *both* guide us, to inhabit the full spectrum of our personal and interpersonal neuroendocrine system? Can we dream of ongoing becoming, as the world ends?

> If it all comes to nothing in the end,
> how can we make nothing
> our very good friend?

TURNING AND RETURNING:
HARVEST AND INTEGRATION

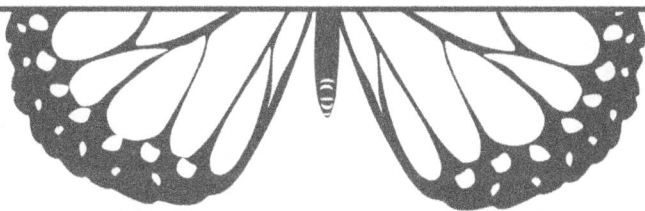

*fighting capitalism and colonialism
with our wild imaginations,
loving touch and daring dreams*

TIME TO CONSIDER

At the end of December through the first week of January, there is a special time. It's time I want to spend integrating what the past year has been, and considering what comes next. As I am focusing on integration and preparation for the year to come, I feel I am following the earth's own rhythm.

Earth's orbit is elliptical in shape. The distance between earth and sun varies throughout the year. During the last week of December and the first week of January, earth travels closer and closer to the sun (coming about 1.6 million miles closer to the sun than the average 93 million miles distance). If the planet were to keep on following its longing for belonging, it would hurtle into the sun, becoming one with it. Instead, it speeds up, rushes by, and stays differentiated.

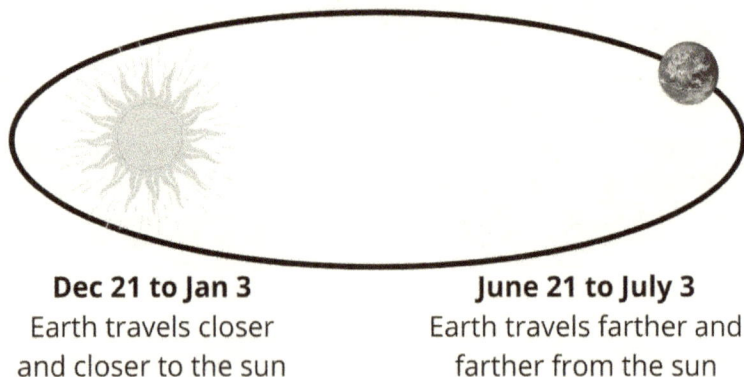

Dec 21 to Jan 3
Earth travels closer
and closer to the sun

June 21 to July 3
Earth travels farther and
farther from the sun

Diagram showing elliptical form of earth's orbit around the sun

At the end of June, and during the first week of July, there is another precious time. During these summer days, earth travels farther and farther away from the sun (coming 1.6 million miles farther away from the sun than the average

93 million miles distance). If earth kept following its longing for differentiation, without returning to love, the planet would leave the solar system. It would disappear on its own trajectory, into cold, almost-empty space. Instead, it slows down, turns around, and stays in relationship.

I want to take time, during these precious times, to consider my path. I review the steps of ecstatic belonging, and notice: What am I harvesting and integrating in each step I am taking, simultaneously and sequentially? How am I doing, in my commitment to walking a medicine path of embodied love?

1. I belong to my own soul. I surrender to the ever-emerging truth of me. I know it and grow it.
2. I belong to those I love. I practice welcoming and cherishing them, including their unlovable parts.
3. I want ecstasy, and I commit to belonging to my longing.
4. I belong to the biosphere that lives through me.
5. I belong to repair. I commit to repairing harm I have done, whether intentionally or unintentionally. I commit to repairing harm done to me.
6. I belong to nonbeing. I integrate spaciousness, as I weave my self into the web of life and death.

What am I feeling, in the simultaneous and sequential practice of these steps?

What is this practice of fighting capitalism and colonialism with our wild imaginations, loving touch and daring dreams?

After we have checked in with ourselves, let's check in with each other.

I welcome one-one connection through the contact form on my website at **EcstaticBelonging.com**.

ACKNOWLEDGEMENTS

I feel and find ecstatic belonging in intimacies with the more than human world, and with precious human souls. This book, and these understandings and practices, emerged in my loving relationships with Doug Wahlsten, Tricia Bowler, Sophia Faria, Leisbeth Van Rompenay, Paula Stromberg, Wendy Baxter, Tom Baxter, Barry Carl, Greta Jane, Max Tea, Daniel Elliott and other dear friends.

The Welcome Home practice was developed with Tricia Bowler and Michael Haines. The Apology Ritual originated with Tricia Bowler. The map for Generative Conflict was conceived together with her, and it grew into its present form in conversation with Kai Cheng Thom, and colleagues and friends at the Institute for the Study of Somatic Sex Education. The chapter on "Belonging to Repair" was in part inspired by Tricia and Michael's work at the Being Held Institute, and our work to address conflict with embodied love inside the community of practice at the Institute. I feel great gratitude for every member of the Queer Transformative Justice Group convened by Kai Cheng Thom and Carly Boyce in 2020 and 2021. Soul Mapping and Relationship Mapping are inspired by Pod Mapping, which is the work of Mia Mingus at the Bay Area Transformative Justice Collective. I am also drawing on the teaching of Wendy Baxter on values-based organizing. I followed the design of Tricia Bowler's "Grace of Existence" program in designing this yearlong practice. Max Tea and I co-wrote "Belonging: A Queer Manifesto" in 2021, and our co-creation was a cauldron in which these ideas got cooked. I am inspired by the people coming together in Rooted Global Village.

I honour the ongoing guidance of my three decades in 12-step recovery programs, along with the sacred ritual use of entheogens and empathogens.

BIBLIOGRAPHY

Aldaz, S., Escudero, L.M., 2010. Imaginal discs. Current Biology 20, R429–R431. https://doi. org/10.1016/j.cub.2010.03.010

brown, adrienne maree, *Emergent Strategy: Shaping Change, Changing Worlds*, AK Press, 2017

Carhart-Harris, R., Leech, R., Hellyer, P., Shanahan, M., Feilding, A., Tagliazucchi, E., Chialvo, D., Nutt, D., 2014. The entropic brain: a theory of conscious states informed by neuroimaging research with psychedelic drugs. Frontiers in Human Neuroscience 8, 20. https://doi.org/10.3389/ fnhum.2014.00020

Chialvo, D.R., 2010. Emergent complex neural dynamics. https://doi.org/10.1038/nphys1803

Elert, Glenn, Music and Noise, The Physics Hypertextbook, https://physics.info/music/

Edsinger E, Dölen G. A Conserved Role for Serotonergic Neurotransmission in Mediating Social Behavior in Octopus. Curr Biol. 2018;28(19):3136-3142.e4. doi:10.1016/j.cub.2018.07.061

Kaba, Mariame and Shira Hassan, *Fumbling Towards Repair: A Workbook for Community Accountability Facilitators*, June 2019

Menakem, Resmaa, 2017. My grandmother's hands: racialized trauma and the pathway to mending our hearts and bodies. Las Vegas: Central Recovery Press.

Nardou, R., Lewis, E.M., Rothhaas, R., Xu, R., Yang, A., Boyden, E., Dölen, G., 2019a. Oxytocindependent reopening of a social reward learning critical period with MDMA. Nature 569, 116–120. https://doi.org/10.1038/s41586-019-1075-9

Pandele, Emily. "Intro to Quantum Superposition". https://www.linkedin.com/pulse/introquantum-superposition-emily-pandele?trk=public_profile_article_view

Pritchard, W.S., 1992. The brain in fractal time: 1/f-like power spectrum scaling of the human electroencephalogram. Int J Neurosci 66, 119–129. https://doi.org/10.3109/00207459208999796

Schick, K., Verveen, A.A., 1974. 1/f noise with a low frequency white noise limit. Nature 251, 599–601. https://doi.org/10.1038/251599a0

Simard, Suzanne, *Finding the Mother Tree: Discovering the Wisdom of the Forest*, Allen Lane, 2021

Smith, Eric and Harold J. Morowitz, *The Origin and Nature of Life on Earth: The Emergence of the Fourth Geosphere*, Cambridge U. Press, 2016,

Su, Y.-H., Liu, Y.-B., Zhang, X.-S., 2011. Auxin–Cytokinin Interaction Regulates Meristem Development. Mol Plant 4, 616–625. https://doi.org/10.1093/mp/ssr007

Szendro, P, Vincze, G., Szasz, A., 2001. Pink-noise behaviour of biosystems. European biophysics journal : EBJ 30, 227–31. https://doi.org/10.1007/s002490100143

Tennessen, J. M., & Thummel, C. S. (2011). Coordinating growth and maturation - insights from Drosophila. *Current biology* : CB, 21(18), R750–R757. https://doi.org/10.1016/j.cub.2011.06.033

Watkinson, S., 2000. Life after Death: The Importance of Salmon Carcasses to British

Columbia's Watersheds. Arctic 53, 92–96

Wilczek, Frank. Entanglement Made Simple, Quanta Magazine, 2016,
    https://www. quantamagazine.org/entanglement-made-
    simple-20160428/#

Yazar-Klosinski, B.B., Mithoefer, M.C., 2017. Potential Psychiatric Uses for
    MDMA. Clinical

Pharmacology & Therapeutics 101, 194–196. https://doi.org/10.1002/
    cpt.565

CAFFYN JESSE

Caffyn Jesse is a queer elder, sacred intimate and writer who revels in the power and pleasures of the erotic. They are actively exploring connections and intersections between psychedelic medicine, transformative justice, somatic sexual wellness and queer ecology.

Caffyn is the author of many books including *Love and Death in a Queer Universe, Intimacy Educator, Science for Sexual Happiness, Orientation: Mapping Queer Meanings and Elements of Intimacy.* She offers an online program in the Art and Science of Sacred Intimacy. See her website EcstaticBelonging.com for many free and low-cost offerings. They are now retired from a longtime role as a teacher of somatic sex education.

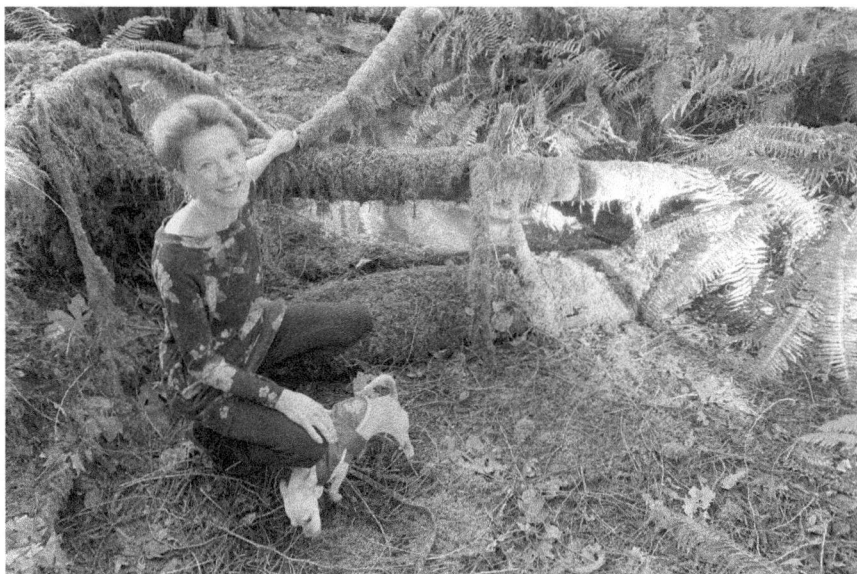

Caffyn with Peeka, photo by Paula Stromberg